★
ICONS

50ˢ FASHION

VINTAGE FASHION AND BEAUTY ADS

Ed. Jim Heimann

Introduction by Laura Schooling

TASCHEN

HONG KONG KÖLN LONDON LOS ANGELES MADRID PARIS TOKYO

Front cover: *Jantzen, 1956*
Back cover: *Arrow Shirts, 1950*
Endpapers: *Van Heusen, 1950*
Facing title page: *J.C. Penney Company, Inc., 1956*
Inside back page: *Chemstrand Corporation, 1955*

**Dates in captions refer to the year of the advertisement's publication and not
necessarily the year in which the product was manufactured.**

To stay informed about upcoming TASCHEN titles, please request our magazine
at www.taschen.com/magazine or write to TASCHEN, Hohenzollernring 53,
D-50672 Cologne, Germany, contact@taschen.com, Fax: +49-221-254919.
We will be happy to send you a free copy of our magazine which is filled with
information about all of our books.

© 2007 TASCHEN GmbH
Hohenzollernring 53, D-50672 Köln
www.taschen.com

Design and editorial coordination: Stephen Schmidt / Duuplex, San Mateo
Design assistants: Sophia Valko, Moss Beach and Gui Zong, Foster City
Production: Morgan Slade, Los Angeles
Project management: Nina Wiener, Los Angeles
German translation: Henriette Zeltner, Munich
French translation: Alice Pétillot, Paris
Multilingual production: www.arnaudbriand.com, Paris

Printed in Italy
ISBN 978-3-8228-4933-0

The New Perfection

By Laura Schooling

After World War II the United States reveled in the glow of victory, togetherness, and an economic boom, and fashion topped off this visage of perfection. Women never left the house without full makeup, coiffed hair, and an army of undergarments, while men also kept up with the Joneses in Italian-inspired three-button suits and a weekend wardrobe for leisure pursuits. There was an appropriate ensemble for every activity and subculture—from sock hops and poodle skirts to biker gangs and motorcycle jackets.

Television shows like *Father Knows Best* and *Leave It to Beaver* projected the ideal American family, while sex became a hot topic of conversation thanks to the Kinsey Reports and the 1953 debut of *Playboy*, featuring Marilyn Monroe as its first centerfold. Men and women read articles about how to impress the opposite sex, with fashion and grooming taking center stage. Frank Sinatra was the epitome of the winsome bachelor—accessorizing with a girl on each arm and donning a knife-sharp suit. While men could transition from the office to a cocktail party without changing their outfit, the womenswear market introduced new garments that were between day- and eveningwear. Cocktail dresses, which were shorter and less formal than evening dresses, allowed women to show off a burgeoning sexual confidence and became must-have party apparel.

The female silhouette, as shaped by clothes, changed dramatically postwar. Christian Dior's first couture collection in 1947 featured the "Bar" suit, which was defined by a structured jacket, tightly cinched at the waist, that blossomed into a full, swinging skirt. Using extra fabric for pure aesthetic at a time when rations were a recent memory was seen by many as an affront to national patriotism, but others delighted in the showy romanticism of these new designs. Carmel Snow, the editor-in-chief of *Harper's Bazaar*, declared this line the "New Look," and by the early fifties the full skirt was being widely copied and mass-produced. Each season, designer clothing had a definitive shape and outline, sending women back to the stores every few months to stay in style. In 1954 Dior introduced the A-line, which might have included a wide and billowy jacket with a slim-fitting skirt, or a ballooning coat that covered a circle skirt. Variations seemed endless in this time of experimentation.

Whatever the style, fabric was used to adorn women's bodies rather than merely cover them. One of the most notable figures to emerge was the hourglass shape—defined by a well-fed plumpness to the flesh and severely contrasted by a tiny waist—which would go on to become the most recognizable female ideal. This look was best observed in women's swimwear, which often consisted of a shell-shaped bust and a tightly cinched waist with fabric curving over the hips. American bombshells Jayne Mansfield and Marilyn Monroe naturally possessed the buxom voluptuousness that other women had to fuss and finagle to achieve. It's no wonder that the first sugar-free soft drink, No-Cal ginger ale, was launched in 1952. And what couldn't be achieved with dieting was helped along by undergarments. Push-up bras formed

Top: *Avon, 1957*   Bottom: *McGregor, 1954*

to a point, and when worn with waist girdles and boned corsets they helped accentuate a large bust and small waist. By 1953 stiletto heels had become popular and further elongated a woman's body. It was perhaps the most torturous, and most enduring, trend to emerge from the fifties.

European women remained faithful to haute couture, thanks to the inspiring designs of Christian Dior and Cristobal Balenciaga and the reemergence in 1954 of Chanel. These designer fashions were reappropriated by fashionable department stores such as Henri Bendel under a house label. For those who still found these fashions too expensive, they were finally able to buy a piece of the glamour as many designers began to license their names to accessory and perfume manufacturers. Now a woman could dress up her nondesigner dress with gloves, a hat, and a purse that carried name cachet.

Menswear began to catch up with womenswear and subtly change with the seasons thanks to the advent of menswear shows in the early fifties. Sporty three-quarter-length car and scooter coats made their way from Italy and Paris to England and the United States, giving men European bragging rights. Menswear became more daring, introducing colored shirts and elaborately patterned and flamboyant ties and socks, and elevating certain accessories to status symbols like cuff links, watches, and briefcases. Clothing from menswear designers such as Brioni and Cerruti possessed a sophistication that lent an air of prestige to its wearer, delivering the same kind of status that European designers had conferred to women. With members of the Rat Pack for inspiration, men's apparel developed a certain flair, which was readily apparent in their hats. With hats for the office, evening, and weekends, the wearer may have found more reasons for a courtesy tip of the brim to the fairer sex.

While glamour was still important, many people began to favor clothes that allowed for more freedom of movement. Even Coco Chanel, the embodiment of prim and proper, criticized the New Look for its restricting fit. She offered refinement and ease of movement in her signature skirt suits. It was this move toward comfort that spawned a number of looks: skirts with built-in bloomers, slip-on sandals, Capri pants, and jeans—the pinnacle of comfort. French actress Brigitte Bardot was undoubtedly one of the sexiest women of the decade, but she was as well-known for her casual attire. She often opted to play down her glamour by dressing her buxom figure in pedal pushers and cotton sundresses, which were perfect for her famous beachside photo ops. Her breezy style was epitomized by the gingham dress she wore to her 1959 wedding.

Menswear benefited from casual use as well. As leisure time increased, clothing for the weekend golfer, swimmer, and boating aficionado filled men's wardrobes. Minimum-care garments became popular, and lightweight textiles allowed for a more relaxed fit. During summertime, men might barbecue in straight-fit, untucked shirts and chinos. Jeans infiltrated the streets thanks to male icons like bad-boy actors James Dean and Marlon Brando. Teenage girls also embraced the look, wearing their jeans loose and cuffed at the bottom and often paired with saddle shoes. Denim did not have an easy time breaking into the mainstream, perhaps because a conservative older generation closely associated them with youth rebellion.

The beatniks represented an equally threatening counterculture but perhaps less so when they were becomingly portrayed by Audrey Hepburn in 1957's *Funny Face*, a movie that humorously reconciles the fashion world's insatiable need for new talent—from both model and designer. Inspired by photographer Richard Avedon and legendary *Harper's Bazaar* editor Diana Vreeland, the film features Hepburn as a pixie-sized beatnik in black leggings, boat-neck shirt, bold eyebrows, and a tight ponytail. While the actress danced to impromptu jazz sessions in Parisian cafés, rock 'n' roll was the main soundtrack for fifties' youth culture.

The sound reached new popularity in 1955 when the Comets' "Rock Around the Clock" spent eight consecutive weeks atop the Billboard charts—teenagers wore their trousers loose so they could move freely on the dance floor. Full skirts enhanced by nylon petticoats were a welcome alternative to stiff crinolines, giving girls extra flair as they twirled and a bit of modesty as they kicked up their legs while doing the jitterbug. Cat-eye glasses were now fashionable, and bubblegum was popped flirtatiously by both genders. Men greased their hair with pomade to keep it in place, often combing it back and flipping it over in a pompadour like Elvis Presley or Johnny Cash. Girls also added volume to their hair, using large rollers to create face-framing waves, or they wore their long hair tussled and messy. When hats were worn, they were often a small accessory—either an unobtrusive flat or slightly rounded cap or a headpiece that could be stuck into the hair with a comb or band.

One of the tiniest accessories of the decade hit the shelves in 1959 when Mattel introduced Barbie, who was dressed in reproductions of the day's most popular looks. With her exaggerated hourglass figure, Barbie quickly became an icon of American childhood and a plastic embodiment of the feminine ideal.

Die neue Perfektion

Von Laura Schooling

Nach dem II. Weltkrieg sonnten sich die USA im Glanz des Sieges, man genoss das Zusammengehörigkeitsgefühl und die Vorzüge des Wirtschaftsbooms. Und natürlich musste auch die Mode zu diesem perfekten Bild passen. Frauen verließen das Haus nie ohne komplettes Make-up, wohl frisiertes Haar und ein ganzes Arsenal an Unterwäsche. Auch die Männer versuchten mitzuhalten und trugen dreiteilige Anzüge im italienischen Stil sowie Freizeitkleidung am Wochenende. Es gab eine passende Kombination für alle möglichen Aktivitäten: von Pudelröcken zum Rock'n'Roll-Tanzen bis hin zu Lederjacken für die Motorradgangs.

Fernsehserien wie *Vater ist der Beste* und *Erwachsen müsste man sein* präsentierten die ideale amerikanische Familie. Gleichzeitig sorgten die Kinsey-Reporte und 1953 das *Playboy*-Debüt – mit Marilyn Monroe als erstem Centerfold – dafür, dass Sex Gesprächsthema wurde. Männer wie Frauen lasen Artikel darüber, wie das andere Geschlecht zu beeindrucken sei, in denen Mode und Styling die Hauptrolle spielten. Frank Sinatra war der Inbegriff des charmanten Junggesellen. Zu seiner Grundausstattung zählten ein Mädchen in jedem Arm und ein messerscharf gebügelter Anzug. Während die Herren direkt vom Büro auf die Cocktailparty gehen konnten, ohne sich vorher umziehen zu müssen, brachte die Damenkonfektion neue Kleidungsstücke auf den Markt, die ein Mittelding zwischen Tages- und Abendmode darstellten. Cocktailkleider waren kürzer und nicht so förmlich wie ein Abendkleid. Sie erlaubten den Damen, ihr aufkeimendes sexuelles Selbstvertrauen zu zeigen und wurden zu unverzichtbaren Partybegleitern.

Die von der Kleidung geformte weibliche Silhouette änderte sich in der Nachkriegszeit auf geradezu dramatische Weise. Christian Diors erste Couture-Kollektion von 1947 zeigte das Kostüm »Bar«, bestehend aus einer figurbetonten, extrem taillierten Jacke und einem weit schwingenden Rock. Der ungeheure Stoffverbrauch aus rein ästhetischen Gründen, und das zu einer Zeit, in der den Menschen Rationierungen noch gut im Gedächtnis waren, wurde von vielen als unpatriotischer Affront aufgefasst. Andere erfreuten sich an der prächtigen Romantik dieser neuen Kreationen. Carmel Snow, die Herausgeberin von *Harper's Bazaar*, erklärte diesen Stil zum »New Look«, und schon Anfang der 1950er-Jahre wurde der weite Rock vielfach kopiert und massenproduziert. In jeder Saison propagierte die Designermode neue Schnitte und Entwürfe, sodass die Damenwelt alle paar Monate in die Geschäfte strömen musste, wenn sie modisch en vogue bleiben wollte. 1954 führte Dior die A-Linie ein, zu der beispielsweise eine weite bauschige Jacke und ein figurbetonter Rock gehörten oder ein ballonförmiger Mantel über einem Tellerrock. Die Variationsmöglichkeiten in dieser experimentierfreudigen Zeit schienen unendlich zu sein.

Egal, welchem Trend man folgte: Stoff war dazu gemacht, den weiblichen Körper zu schmücken, anstatt ihn nur zu verhüllen. Eine der auffälligsten Silhouetten war die Sanduhr-Figur – üppige, weibliche Formen und im Kontrast

Top: *After Six by Rudofker, 1955*   Bottom: *Catalina, 1952*

dazu eine winzige Taille –, die sich zum weiblichen Schönheitsideal schlechthin entwickeln sollte. Am deutlichsten zeigte sich dieser Look in der Bademode, die oft aus einem muschelförmigen Oberteil, einer eng geschnürten Taille und Stoff, der sich an die Hüften schmiegte, bestand. Amerikanische Sexbomben wie Jayne Mansfield und Marilyn Monroe besaßen von Natur aus jene dralle Üppigkeit, die andere Frauen nur mit großem Aufwand und viel Schummelei erzielten. Kein Wunder also, dass 1952 mit No-Cal Ginger Ale die erste zuckerfreie Limonade auf den Markt kam. Und was sich durch keine Diät erreichen ließ, musste die Unterwäsche richten. Push-up-BHs formten einen spitzen Busen, und wenn man sie zu Hüfthaltern und Fischbein-Corsagen trug, konnte man eine große Oberweite und eine schmale Taille zur Schau stellen. 1953 hatten sich auch die Stilettos durchgesetzt und verstärkten die optische Streckung der weiblichen Silhouette – sicherlich der qualvollste und zugleich dauerhafteste Trend der Fifties.

Europäerinnen setzten dank der inspirierenden Kreationen von Christian Dior, Cristobal Balenciaga und der Wiedereröffnung des Hauses Chanel im Jahr 1954 weiterhin auf Haute Couture. Diese Designermode wurden von renommierten Warenhäusern wie Henri Bendel im Rahmen eigener Labels aufgegriffen. Wem auch diese Kleider zu teuer waren, konnte sich wenigstens ein bisschen Glamour in Form von Accessoires und Parfums leisten, da viele Designer damit begannen, entsprechende Lizenzen zu vergeben. Nun konnte eine Frau ein No-Name-Kleid durch Handschuhe, einen Hut und eine Handtasche mit prestigeträchtigen Namen aufwerten.

Auch die Herrenmode begann langsam aufzuholen und pro Saison ein wenig zu variieren – nicht zuletzt auch aufgrund der Einführung von eigenen Modenschauen in den frühen 1950er-Jahren. Sportliche, dreiviertellange Mäntel für Auto- und Motorrollerfahrer bahnten sich ihren Weg von Italien und Paris bis nach England und schließlich Amerika, wo sich die Männer voller Stolz europäisch gaben. Die Herrenmode wurde generell gewagter. Sie propagierte farbige Hemden, raffiniert gemusterte, auffällige Krawatten und Socken sowie Accessoires, die zu regelrechten Statussymbolen wurden wie etwa Manschettenknöpfe, Uhren und Aktentaschen. Kleidung von Herrenmodedesignern wie Brioni und Cerruti besaß eine Eleganz, die ihrem Träger das gleiche Prestige gab, das europäische Modeschöpfer den Damen längst verliehen hatten. Inspiriert von den Mitgliedern des »Rat Pack« entwickelte die Herrenbekleidung einen ganz bestimmten Look, der besonders in den Hüten zum Ausdruck kam. Es gab Hüte fürs Büro, für den Abend und fürs Wochenende, sodass ihre Träger nie um einen Anlass verlegen waren, sich angesichts einer schönen Frau ehrerbietig an die Krempe zu tippen.

Glamour spielte zwar noch eine wichtige Rolle, aber immer mehr Menschen begannen eine Mode zu bevorzugen, die ihnen größere Bewegungsfreiheit bot. Selbst Coco Chanel, der Inbegriff der Eleganz, kritisierte den zu engen Sitz des New Look. Mit ihren unverwechselbaren Kostümen bot sie Raffinesse und Komfort zugleich. Es war dieser Schritt in Richtung Bequemlichkeit, der eine ganze Reihe von Looks hervorbrachte: Hosenröcke, Sandaletten, Caprihosen und Jeans – der Gipfel an Lässigkeit. Die französische Schauspielerin Brigitte Bardot war zweifellos eine der attraktivsten Frauen jenes Jahrzehnts, aber sie war auch berühmt für ihre legeren Outfits. Oft spielte sie ihren Glamour herunter, indem sie ihre üppige Figur in Dreiviertelhosen und Baumwollkleidchen präsentierte, die für ihre berühmten

Above: *Van Heusen, 1956*

Fotosessions am Strand perfekt geeignet waren. Der Inbegriff ihres lässigen Stils war das Gingham-Kleid, das sie 1959 zu ihrer Hochzeit trug.

Auch die Herrenmode profitierte vom Trend zum Legeren. Da immer mehr freie Zeit zur Verfügung stand, waren die Schränke mit Kleidung für Wochenendgolfer, -schwimmer und -segler gefüllt. Pflegeleichtes war gefragt und leichte Stoffe, die locker saßen. Im Sommer standen die Herren der Schöpfung in gerade geschnittenen, über der Baumwollhose getragenen Hemden am Grill. Dank männlicher Idole wie den »Bad Boys« James Dean und Marlon Brando wurden Jeans im Straßenbild immer häufiger. Auch weibliche Teenager griffen diesen Look auf, trugen weite, hochgekrempelte Jeans und Sattelschuhe. Bis Denim jedoch auch für die breite Masse tragbar wurde, sollte es noch eine Weile dauern, da ihn die konservative ältere Generation mit jugendlicher Rebellion verband.

Auch die Beatniks standen für eine als bedrohlich empfundene Gegenkultur. Das sollte sich jedoch ändern, nachdem Audrey Hepburn sie 1957 in *Ein süßer Fratz* positiv porträtiert hatte. Der Film schildert auf humorvolle, versöhnliche Weise den unstillbaren Bedarf der Modewelt nach neuen Talenten – nach Models ebenso wie Designern. Inspiriert vom Fotografen Richard Avedon und der legendären Chefredakteurin von *Harper's Bazaar*, Diana Vreeland, zeigt der Film die Hepburn als eine Art Beatnik-Elfe, mit schwarzen Leggings, Shirts mit U-Boot-Ausschnitt, betonten Augenbrauen und einem streng gebundenem Pferdeschwanz. Während die Schauspielerin in Pariser Cafés zu improvisierten Jazz-Sessions tanzte, bestand der Soundtrack der Jugendkultur in den 1950er-Jahren hauptsächlich aus Rock'n'Roll.

Zu neuer Popularität gelangte diese Musik, als die Comets 1955 mit »Rock Around the Clock« acht Wochen in Folge an der Spitze der Billboard-Charts standen. Teenager trugen damals locker sitzende Hosen, um sich auf dem Tanzparkett ungehindert bewegen zu können. Weite Röcke, die durch Petticoats aus Nylon zusätzlich betont wurden, waren eine willkommene Alternative zu steifen Reifröcken. Sie verliehen den Mädchen einen besonderen Charme, wenn sie herumwirbelten und sorgten für ein bisschen Anstand, wenn sie beim Jitterbug die Beine in die Luft warfen. Schmetterlingsbrillen waren ebenfalls in Mode, und Jugendliche beiderlei Geschlechts ließen kokett Kaugummiblasen platzen. Die Herren fixierten ihre Frisuren mit Pomade und kämmten ihr Haar wie Elvis Presley oder Johnny Cash zur Tolle. Auch die Damen verhalfen ihren Frisuren mithilfe von Lockenwicklern zu mehr Volumen. Oder aber sie trugen ihr langes Haar offen und leicht verstrubbelt. Wenn sie überhaupt Hüte aufsetzten, dann meist kleine Accessoires wie flache oder leicht gewölbte Kappen oder Kopfbedeckungen, die mit einem Kamm oder Band in den Haaren befestigt wurden.

Eines des winzigsten Accessoires dieses Jahrzehnts kam 1959 in die Regale, als Mattel seine Barbie auf den Markt brachte. Sie trug die jeweils aktuellen Looks im Miniformat. Mit ihrer übertriebenen Sanduhr-Figur wurde die Barbiepuppe rasch zu einer Ikone der amerikanischen Kindheit und zur Plastikverkörperung des weiblichen Ideals.

Above: *Minnesota Wollen, 1959*

La nouvelle perfection

Par Laura Schooling

Après la Seconde Guerre mondiale, les États-Unis, tout auréolés de la victoire, savourent le sentiment d'unité nationale et les bienfaits du boom économique... et la mode vient mettre une touche finale à cette image de perfection. Les femmes ne quittent pas leur maison sans un maquillage impeccable, une coiffure soignée et une kyrielle de sous-vêtements, et les hommes ne sont pas en reste avec leurs costumes trois boutons d'inspiration italienne et leur garde-robe destinée aux loisirs du week-end. Il existe une tenue spécifique pour chaque divertissement ou activité depuis la *poodle skirt* – jupe bouffante à mi-mollet – des soirées « Sock Hops » au blouson de cuir des bandes de motards.

Les séries télévisées comme *Papa a raison* (*Father Knows Best*) et *Leave It to Beaver* projettent l'image d'une famille américaine idéale, tandis que le sexe devient un sujet de conversation brûlant grâce aux Rapports Kinsey et au lancement, en 1953, de *Playboy*, avec Marilyn Monroe comme première pin up de magazine. Dans ces publications, les hommes comme les femmes trouvent de précieux conseils pour faire impression sur le sexe opposé, tandis que la mode et les soins de beauté y occupent une place prépondérante. Frank Sinatra est alors l'exemple même du charmant célibataire, dont les accessoires fétiches sont une jolie fille à chaque bras et un costume impeccablement taillé. Si les hommes peuvent passer du bureau au cocktail mondain sans se changer, le prêt-à-porter féminin voit naître une nouvelle tenue, entre mode de jour et mode du soir : plus courte et moins formelle que la robe du soir, la robe de cocktail permet aux femmes de jouer de leur assurance sexuelle fraîchement acquise et devient un vêtement incontournable en bonne société.

La silhouette féminine, façonnée par le vêtement, change radicalement au lendemain de la guerre. La première collection haute couture de Christian Dior, en 1947, présente l'ensemble « Bar », caractérisé par une veste structurée qui prend étroitement la taille pour ensuite s'évaser en une jupe ample et ondulante. Beaucoup jugent qu'utiliser autant de tissu supplémentaire dans un souci purement esthétique alors que le rationnement est encore dans toutes les mémoires constitue un affront au patriotisme américain, mais d'autres raffolent du romantisme extravagant de ce nouveau costume. Carmel Snow, directrice de *Harper's Bazaar*, baptise ce style le « New Look » et, au début des années 1950, la jupe ample est largement copiée, notamment par la grande distribution. Chaque saison, les créations de couturiers ont une forme et une silhouette nouvelles, qui oblige les femmes à courir les boutiques pour renouveler leur garde-robe. En 1954, Dior présente la ligne « A » avec, entre autres, une large veste gonflée associée à une jupe près du corps, ou encore un manteau bouffant couvrant une jupe évasée et ample. En ces temps d'expérimentation tous azimuts, les variations semblent infinies.

Quel que soit le style choisi, le tissu orne le corps de la femme plus qu'il ne le couvre. Parmi les silhouettes qui naissent au cours de cette période, une des plus marquantes est celle du sablier, où l'opulence des formes du corps contraste radicalement avec la finesse de la taille, et qui deviendra l'idéal féminin

Top: *American Optical, 1959*   Bottom: *Dickies, 1955*

le plus reconnaissable. Cette allure est particulièrement présente dans les lignes de maillots de bain, qui propulsent le buste en avant, ceignent étroitement la taille et viennent draper les hanches. Les bombes sexuelles américaines comme Jayne Mansfield et Marilyn Monroe sont naturellement dotées de cette généreuse volupté que tant d'autres femmes ne peuvent qu'envier. Rien d'étonnant à ce que la première boisson non alcoolisée sans sucre, la No-Cal Ginger Ale, ait été lancée en 1952. Si elle ne parviennent pas à atteindre les formes convoitées par le régime, les femmes peuvent désormais compter sur de nouveaux artifices : les soutiens-gorge pigeonnants font pointer la poitrine en obus et, portés avec gaines et corsets baleinés, ils accentuent l'ampleur du buste et la petitesse de la taille. En 1953, le talon aiguille, très populaire, allonge encore la silhouette féminine. Cette tendance a sans doute été à la fois la plus douloureuse et la plus tenace de celles qui sont nées au cours des années 1950.

Les femmes européennes restent fidèles à la haute couture, grâce à la qualité des modèles de Christian Dior ou de Cristobal Balenciaga et à la réémergence de Chanel en 1954. Les silhouettes parisiennes sont reprises sous des marques maison par des grands magasins à la mode comme Henri Bendel. Celles pour lesquelles ces modèles sont encore trop onéreux peuvent malgré tout s'offrir des pépites de glamour, un grand nombre de couturiers commençant à donner leur nom à des accessoires où à des parfums. Une femme peut désormais porter une robe sans marque avec des gants, un chapeau et un sac griffés par les plus grands.

La mode masculine marche dans les pas de la mode féminine et évolue subrepticement au fil des saisons grâce à l'organisation de défilés de mode masculins au début de la décennie. Les vestes trois-quarts sport et les blousons de scooter partent d'Italie vers Paris pour gagner l'Angleterre puis les États-Unis, où ils confèrent aux hommes un statut de matamore à l'européenne. La mode masculine devient plus audacieuse, ose les chemises colorées, l'extravagance de cravates et de chaussettes à motifs complexes et élève les accessoires comme les boutons de manchette, les montres ou les mallettes au rang de signes extérieurs de richesse. La sophistication des vêtements pour hommes créés par Brioni ou Cerruti confère allure et prestige à ceux qui les portent, à l'image de ce qu'avaient fait les couturiers européens pour rehausser l'élégance des femmes. Puisant son inspiration auprès des membres du Rat Pack, l'habillement masculin se découvre une nouvelle allure, qui transparaît déjà dans la vogue des chapeaux. Qu'ils soient destinés au bureau, aux sorties mondaines ou au week-end, ils fournissent aux hommes autant d'occasions de signifier leur admiration au beau sexe par un signe discret.

Bien que l'élégance soit toujours importante, les vêtements qui accordent une plus grande liberté de mouvement trouvent un écho de plus en plus large. Même Coco Chanel, incarnation de l'élégance et du bon ton, critique la coupe trop contraignante du New Look. Elle y oppose le raffinement et le confort des tailleurs qui feront sa gloire. Cette recherche de l'aisance physique lance une myriade de styles : jupes avec culotte bouffante intégrée, sandales à enfiler, pantalons capri et, summum du confort, le jean. Brigitte Bardot est sans aucun doute la femme la plus sexy de la décennie, mais elle est également réputée pour la simplicité de sa garde-robe. Elle choisit souvent de modérer l'effet de ses formes généreuses en adoptant robes d'été en coton et corsaires, parfaits pour ses fameuses séances de photo en bord de mer. Son allure naturelle atteint un paroxysme avec la robe vichy qu'elle porte pour son mariage, en 1959.

La mode masculine n'échappe pas non plus à cette tendance à la décontraction. À mesure que le temps de loisirs augmente, la garde-robe des hommes se remplit de tenues destinées à l'amateur de golf, de natation ou de voile. Le goût du public se porte sur les vêtements qui nécessitent peu d'entretien et les tissus légers qui permettent des coupes plus décontractées. Pendant l'été, l'homme peut s'occuper du barbecue avec une chemise à manches courtes tombant sur un pantalon en toile. Les jeans envahissent la rue grâce à des idoles masculines comme les acteurs rebelles James Dean et Marlon Brando. Les adolescentes se saisissent aussi de cette tendance en portant leurs jeans larges et resserrés à la cheville, souvent avec des chaussures basses bicolores. Le denim ne devient grand public que difficilement, peut-être parce que l'ancienne génération, conservatrice, l'associait étroitement à la jeunesse en rébellion.

Les beatniks représentent une contre-culture tout aussi menaçante mais sans doute de façon plus charmante lorsqu'elle est incarnée par Audrey Hepburn dans *Drôle de frimousse*, en 1957 – un film humoristique sur la soif insatiable du monde de la mode pour les nouveaux talents, du point de vue du modèle et du créateur. Le film s'inspire de la vie du photographe Richard Avedon et de la célèbre rédactrice en chef du *Harper's Bazaar*, Diana Vreeland, et présente une Audrey Hepburn en beatnik miniature, arborant caleçons noirs, pull à col montant, sourcils graphiques et queue de cheval serrée. Si l'actrice danse sur des improvisations jazzy dans les cafés de Paris, c'est le rock 'n' roll qui constitue la toile de fond sonore de la culture jeune dans les années 1950.

Le rock accède à une nouvelle popularité en 1955, tandis que la chanson des Comets *Rock Around the Clock* reste huit semaines en tête des ventes de disques – les adolescents portent des pantalons larges afin de pouvoir évoluer librement sur la piste de danse. Les jupes pleines dont l'ampleur est accentuée par des jupons de nylon apportent une alternative bienvenue aux rigides crinolines et donnent de l'effet aux tournoiements des filles tout en protégeant leur pudeur lors des acrobaties du jitterbug. Les lunettes étirées en œil de chat sont à la mode et les jeunes représentants des deux sexes mâchent leur chewing-gum d'un air entendu. Les hommes graissent leurs cheveux avec de la pommade pour les faire tenir en place, souvent peignés en arrière et roulés sur le front à la manière d'Elvis Presley ou de Johnny Cash. Les filles aussi donnent du volume à leur coiffure en utilisant de gros rouleaux pour créer des vagues qui viennent encadrer le visage ou portent leurs cheveux crêpés et lâchés à la sauvageonne. Lorsqu'elles portent un chapeau, il est le plus souvent de petite taille – une sorte de calotte très plate ou légèrement bombée ou un accessoire de cheveu qui peut être piqué dans les cheveux avec un peigne ou un bandeau.

Un des les plus petits accessoires de la décennie apparaît en 1959 lorsque Mattel lance sa Barbie, habillée de reproductions des tenues les plus tendance du moment. Avec sa silhouette en sablier exagérée, Barbie devient rapidement une icône enfantine outre-Atlantique ainsi qu'une incarnation de l'idéal féminin.

TRY THIS ON FOR SIGHS!

An Arrow Shirt does something for a guy that does something to the gals.

Maybe they figure any man that's so neatly groomed would be just as neat around the house. Maybe that virile Mitoga-tailored fit.

Or maybe they're sure any man who insists on the "Sanforized" label (fabric shrinkage less than 1%), anchored buttons, and the *value* in every Arrow Shirt is sure to be a good provider! Whatever it is, it's *wonderful!*

The shirt being admired is *Par* (above), soft, spread collar...regular or French cuffs. $3.65. If you like a non-wilt collar, you pick *Dart*, $3.65; *Mall* (in finer broadcloth), $3.95; or *Dale* (premium broadcloth), $4.50. *Drew* has medium-short points, low neckband, $3.65.

Tie Note—These shirts will look even handsomer with Arrow's luxurious new *Royalty Satin Ties* (shown) in popular paisley patterns! $2.00 each.

ARROW SHIRTS and TIES

Cluett, Peabody & Co., Inc., Makers of Arrow Shirts, Ties, Sports Shirts, Handkerchiefs, Underwear.

Hart Schaffner & Marx, 1950 ◀◀   Arrow, 1950   ▶ Arrow, 1951

Wear an Arrow Shirt
and you'll simply sweep
her off her feet!

winning colors

Take the lead this Spring in a suit so new in fabric pattern and color
that it sets the fashion trend of the year, and for some time to come.
That's Futura by Hart Schaffner & Marx. Contrasting touches of
color stand out from subdued backgrounds of tans, grays
or blues, giving a third-dimensional effect to the appearance of
the fabric. It is the sort of suit that will raise your
spirits but not your eyebrows. Most important, whichever model
you choose, it will have that air of distinction so characteristic
of tailoring by Hart Schaffner & Marx.

*This handsome Futura suit is
the 2-button patch pocket version of the new Trend model.*

HART SCHAFFNER & MARX®

Warm & Sunny
When It's Icy Cold

Quality at your feet

BROWN
SHOE COMPANY

you can't tell
the mothers from
the daughters in

*mother-daughter
classics*

Because everybody looks young
and has fun in these easy-living
casuals. And this year we've
given them a sophisticated new
slenderness that mothers and
daughters will *both* look smart in! Why
not try them on together?

Shoes Illustrated
6.95

Other styles, 6.95 to 10.95
Higher Denver West

westports by *life stride*

Life Stride Division, Brown Shoe Company, St. Louis

Borgana, 1951 ◀

Brown Shoe Company, 1951

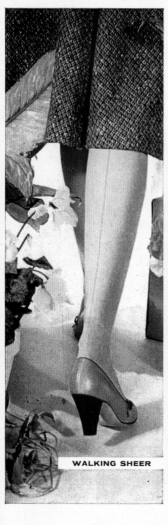

WALKING SHEER

DRESS SHEER

EVENING SHEER

there's a time and a place

for all three sheers...
in today's lovely stockings of Du Pont Nylon

Here's a hint on how to get the most from your stockings. Simply wear the sheer that's right for the occasion. Today's nylons are being made for the uses you'll give them—and sold by use names such as Walking Sheers...Dress Sheers...Evening Sheers. Next time you buy your nylon stockings, remember to buy them to suit the occasion.

Cosmopolitan - the man who wears the Stetson with the Mode Edge

Wherever you are you're right in style wearing a Stetson with the famous Mode Edge. It's a sign of fine craftsmanship for those who demand the custom touch. Here you see the Stetson Sussex with the Mode Edge...a hat designed for the trend towards the slimmer, trimmer silhouette. New smart colors with contrasting bands. The Stetson Sussex—$15. Other Stetson styles with the Mode Edge—$15 and $20.

The STETSON is part of the man

The Stetson "Cushioned-To-Fit" leather has been the standard of hat comfort for over 70 years.

Stetson Hats are made only by John B. Stetson Company, and its affiliated companies throughout the world.

Du Pont, 1956 ◄

Stetson, 1954

HATS—As healthy as they're handsome

THE HAVELOCK—The invention of Sir Henry Havelock of the British Army in India about 1850. Also known as the "kepi" and "forage cap" in other armies. The havelock shown here is worn by a French legionnaire. It's a handsome hat whose primary purpose is protection, to protect the back of the wearer's head and neck from the dangerous direct rays of the tropical sun.

No MATTER WHERE YOU LIVE—in New York or New Caledonia—the purpose of your hat is to protect your eyes from glare, your hair from sun and soot, your head from icy blasts. That's the *primary* purpose of a hat. Don't go bareheaded—it simply isn't a very wise thing to do.

It's unkind to your sinuses, and definitely unkind to the hair on your head. There's a handsome hat waiting to improve your appearance—and to protect your head. Styled in shape and color to the moment, there's a *right* hat for the occasion wherever you go, or play, or work.

"Wear a Hat—It's as Healthy as It's Handsome!"

These fine hat labels have published this advertisement in the interests of good grooming and good health of American men.

 DOBBS CAVANAGH KNOX

BERG BYRON C & K DUNLAP

 *Divisions of the Hat Corporation of America—Makers of Fine Hats for Men and Women*

Hat Corporation of America, 1952

HATS—As healthy as they're handsome

THE "TEN GALLON"—The traditional hat of the Western plains has many functions. Its broad brim keeps glare out of the wearer's eyes and the high crown protects his head from the burning sun. It has been used as pillow, fire-fanner, and drinking cup!

Whether you punch cows or punch a clock, never forget the primary purpose of a hat— to *protect* you. A hat shades your eyes from aching glare, keeps sun and city soot off your hair, and guards your head against icy blasts. That's why when you go bare-headed you're just asking for trouble. It's foolish—especially when there is a handsome, well-styled hat just waiting to improve your appearance. Look in your dealer's window—he has a hat designed *right* for any occasion, wherever you go, or play, or work.

"Wear a Hat—It's as Healthy as It's Handsome!"

These fine hat labels have published this advertisement in the interests of good grooming and good health of American men.

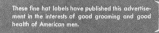 DOBBS CAVANAGH KNOX

BERG BYRON C&K DUNLAP

Divisions of the Hat Corporation of America—Makers of Fine Hats for Men and Women

Hat Corporation of America, 1952

Here's your pal... HOPALONG CASSIDY...
and his <u>brand</u> <u>new</u> cowboy boots!

That's right, boys and girls!... these hand-some new boots are Hoppy's very own! You'll be proud to own them, and you'll really get a lot of fun wearing them!

You'll enjoy their beauty and comfort for a long time, because they are made by the most expert craftmen at Acme, the world's largest makers of cowboy boots! Get your pair right away!

Your Acme dealer has a colorful assortment of these brand new Hopalong Cassidy cowboy boots! See them as soon as you can!

ACME BOOT COMPANY, CLARKSVILLE, TENNESSEE

©"Tested in the stirrup.. where it really counts"

World's largest makers of cowboy boots

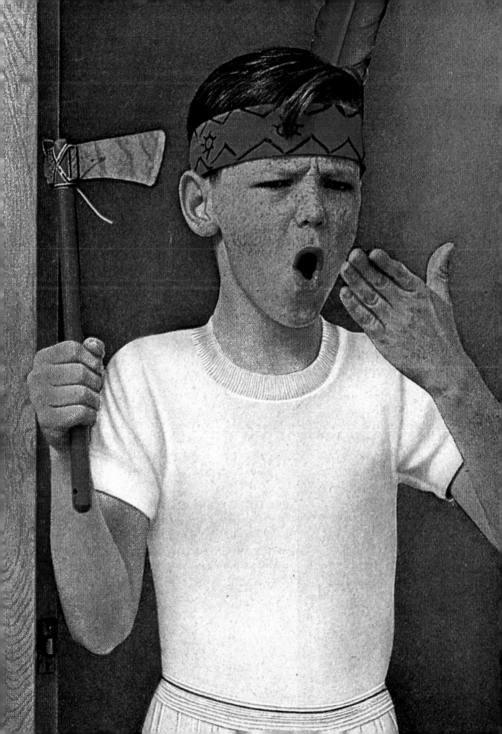

Coopers, 1950

Coopers, 1950

make like a medicine man

...in **Voodoo Shorts**

Munsingwear gives you a chance to show *her* . . . you can be just as wild and original with your shorts as she is with her hats. Primitive designs, mysterious as the jungle. Loud, laughing colors that seem to chant a reckless rhythm. Only Munsingwear brings you these Voodoo Print boxer shorts.

In fine rayon, sizes 30-42. $2

1. **CROMANTI** (jungle dance)—royal blue, red, brown, gray.

2. **DJUKA** (bushman tribe)—gray, maize, green, wine.

3. **VODU** (guardian spirit)—red, gray, maize, royal blue, brown.

4. **GABUN** (primitive masks)—gray, royal blue, brown, red, maize.

MUNSINGWEAR®

at better stores everywhere

P.S. *to the ladies . . . on his day, June 17 . . . give the chief of your tribe Voodoo Print boxer shorts.*

ESQUIRE : June 1951

37

Munsingwear, 1951

make like Nero in...

QUO VADIS shorts

**...speed up the process
by showing your "empress" this page**

A minute after she sees this page she'll
chariot off to buy you Munsingwear's exclusive
QUO VADIS shorts. The gay designs are
plucked right out of the dazzling motion picture of
spectacular Roman days. Poor toga clad Nero
never knew the smart comfort of these full-cut
rayon boxer shorts. They're in the happiest
patterns you ever saw. If she doesn't come
through ... get 'em yourself. $2

*Inspired by M.G.M's great technicolor
motion picture. An authentic QUO VADIS
fashion, exclusive fabric by*
NICKERBOCKER *textile corp*

Eight fiery patterns blazing with color

MUNSINGWEAR®
at better stores everywhere

Munsingwear, 1951

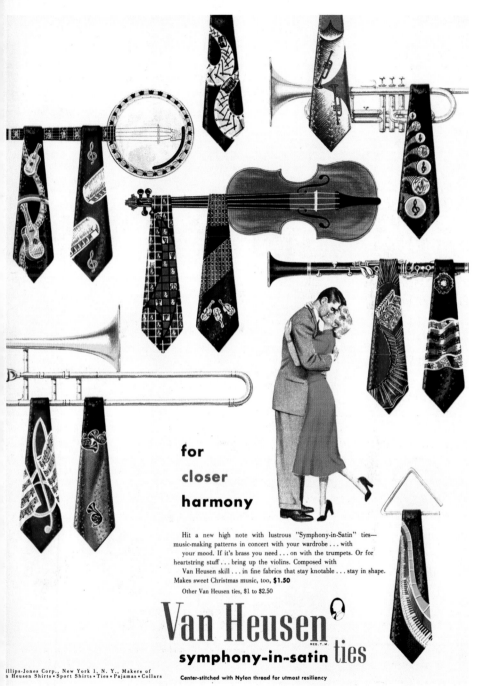

for

closer

harmony

Hit a new high note with lustrous "Symphony-in-Satin" ties—
music-making patterns in concert with your wardrobe . . . with
your mood. If it's brass you need . . . on with the trumpets. Or for
heartstring stuff . . . bring up the violins. Composed with
Van Heusen skill . . . in fine fabrics that stay knotable . . . stay in shape.
Makes sweet Christmas music, too, **$1.50**
Other Van Heusen ties, $1 to $2.50

Van Heusen ties

REG. T. M.

symphony-in-satin

Center-stitched with Nylon thread for utmost resiliency

illips-Jones Corp., New York 1, N. Y., Makers of
n Heusen Shirts • Sport Shirts • Ties • Pajamas • Collars

Designer's Collection

by SWANK

A fabulous assortment of unusual Cuff Links

Split Coin—Actually a pair of extra-size cuff links, $2.50

Amsterdam
$3.50 per pair

Lucky Bug
$3.50 per pair

Hope Stone
$3.50 per pair

Sportrait
$3.50 per pair

Black Magic
$2.50 per pair

Nomad
$2.50 per pair

Steeplechase
$3.50 per pair

Mardi Gras
$3.50 per pair

Primitive
$2.50 per pair

Zebra Stone
$3.50 per pair

Fleur de Lis
$1.50 per pair

Ceramic
$2.50 per pair

Trio
$3.50 per pair

Tiger Stone
$2.50 per pair

Pirate
$3.50 per pair

Chariot
$1.50 per pair

Viking
$2.50 per pair

Gladiator
$3.50 per pair

Bali
$1.50 per pair

Knight
$2.50 per pair

Carousel
$1.50 per pair

Dragon
$2.50 per pair

Charger
$2.50 per pair

Reindeer
$2.50 per pair

Medieval
$2.50 per pair

Street Scene
$2.50 per pair

Sage
$2.50 per pair

All cuff links shown actual size except Split Coin which is slightly reduced. Prices subject to Fed. Tax.

Swank, 1954

"Dress right—you can't afford not to."

There's an Old World Elegance in new "Spanish Mosaics"

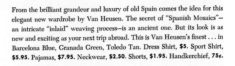

From the brilliant grandeur and luxury of old Spain comes the idea for this elegant new wardrobe by Van Heusen. The secret of "Spanish Mosaics"— an intricate "inlaid" weaving process—is an ancient one. But its look is as new and exciting as your next trip abroad. This is Van Heusen's finest . . . in Barcelona Blue, Granada Green, Toledo Tan. Dress Shirt, **$5.** Sport Shirt, **$5.95.** Pajamas, **$7.95.** Neckwear, **$2.50.** Shorts, **$1.95.** Handkerchief, **75¢.**

Another fashion wardrobe by

VAN HEUSEN®

Van Heusen, 1956

underscore

your fashion

leadership...

FORMAL WEAR in PARFAIT COLORS

After Six
BY RUDOFKER

BLUEBERRY (Blue)
STRAWBERRY (Pink)
GRAPE (Helio)
BANANA (Maize)
FRENCH VANILLA
(Frosty White)
BLACK WALNUT
(Charcoal)

Hark, ye urbane souls who already know many of life's pleasures — there's something new under the moon!... It's Parfait Colors, a fresh and delightful fashion in formal wear. Six ever-so-subtle gentlemen's hues: discreet, dignified. They blend the luxury of Dacron and rayon. (The charcoal is a blend of Silk Shantung and Orlon.) And they are tailored with the fashion authority of "AFTER SIX", world's leading designer and largest maker of formal wear. Priced about **37.50**
slightly higher West of the Rockies and Canada.

Earl-Glo Bemberg Linings
(Cummerbund and tie sets, too, in patterns and Parfait Colors!)

At fine stores everywhere. Write for free dress chart to: **RUDO SUMRWEAR, INC., PHILADELPHIA 3, PA.**

"they say the most flattering things about you . . ."

Inviting . . . as they look!

The moment you ease your feet into a pair of these
cool-looking, wonderful-feeling new City Club Shoes you'll know
you've found something really rare!
With every step you take, you'll treat yourself to glove-like
comfort . . . masterful styling that reflects
over half a century of fine shoe-making craftsmanship . . . that look
of quality you've been paying much, much more to get!

City Club
by Peters   distinctive shoes for men

Ask to see No. 84574 $12⁹⁵*

OTHER CITY CLUB SHOES FROM $8.95 TO $17.95. ALSO MAKERS OF
WESBORO SHOES FOR MEN . . . FROM $6.95 TO $8.95.
* SLIGHTLY HIGHER WEST.

How can a shirt that <u>looks</u> so good <u>feel</u> so good!

The answer's in the collar —the sensational, new *Arafold* Collar! Here's how it works—

You see, Arafold has no seam, no collar band on the inside. This is for smooth comfort!

This amazing collar slopes so low on your neck you feel almost as free-and-easy as this.

Yet, buttoned, with a tie, Arafold is as smart a *looking* collar as you've ever worn!

IT'S ARROW'S NEW REVOLUTIONARY Arafold Collar!

You know how good it feels whe you get home, loosen your tie an unbutton your collar? Man, that comfort! Well, you're practicall that comfortable *all day long* wit Arafold! And you *still* have tha well-groomed Arrow look.

Drop into your Arrow dealer' soon, ask to see Bi-Way with th Arafold Collar. Let him show yo how this supremely comfortabl collar works.

You'll find Arafold in a sprea collar, a long-point collar, a buttor down, a regular-point collar, and rounded-point collar.

Of course, like all Arrow shirt: Bi-Way with the Arafold Collar i "Sanforized"-labeled, will neve shrink out of fit. Buttons are ar chored on to stay. Cluett, Peabody & Co., Inc. Arrow Shirts, Sports Shirt: Ties, Handkerchiefs, Underwear.

ARROW'S
BI-WAY SHIRT
with the new ARAFOLD COLLAR

Wembley *fashions*

Sea, Sand and Sun

FASHION ACADEMY AWARD 1951

"...for originality in design and inspired fashion styling."

$1^{50} - $2

Each beautiful pattern
in six different
Spring color combinations.

For the Man in Her Life

Wembley

®REG. U.S. PAT. OFF.—COPYRIGHT 1951 WEMBLEY, INC.

Wembley Ties are approved for fashion by Men's Fashion Guild • For name of store nearest you, write Wembley, Inc., Empire State Building, New York

23355

23344

23264

23332

23321

om the Necktie Super Market. These remarkable direct olor photographs show 12 style leaders from the mail rder house which sells ties to the business and profesonal men of the U. S. From practically every city nd town men send for ties to Haband in Paterson, N. J. and these 12 are the current favorites. Some have wondered why men send to Paterson year after year for them when other good ties can be bought just around the corner almost anywhere. The answer lies right here in these pictures. Excellent good taste is combined with well chosen patterns and exceptional color-

ing. And more obviously, of course, there are the factors of economy and convenience. All of this is possible, particularly the styling and the economy, because Haband sells absolutely nothing other than neckties—with super intensive concentration upon one quality.

Look the pictures over, leisurely and carefully, and you will find it interesting to discover how neatly the group will fit into your own wardrobe. The pictures are honest. They neither flatter nor harm the product and as such they serve their purpose well, for men can match them up with their suits and shirts in full con-

fidence that there will be no let down when they the actual ties, cut to regulation shape and length fr today's standard rayon fabrics and expertly finished to the last detail. If you would like to get acquainted further with them, you need feel no hesitation in ordering a set, for Haband is vouched for by all usual commercial agencies and is probably known well by many of your friends and neighbors — most certainly by your own Postmaster.

Haband Company, 1950

23229

23276

2329

23324

23328

and
SOLI
COLO
in
NYLO

MAROON —
ROYAL —
NAVY —
BROWN —
GREEN —
BLACK —

Check off or Jot Down the Numbers you would like to wear and send them to the company with your remittance. The ties will reach you by return mail, bringing you a thrill and satisfaction because you will find them more than you expected in body fullness, color depth and dollars and cents value—none of which can be shown in any picture. But, if for any reason you don't want to wear them, you need only send them back to have your money refunded with equal dispatch. Economical handling requires a minimum order of 3 ties. But take 6, a season's supply, and receive with that order a timely gift of a 1951 Easel Type Desk Calendar. Or, with Christmas coming on, take every tie shown (12) plus the Desk Piece for only $13.20.

BUY 6 TIES and get this FREE

ESQUIRE GIRL DESK CALENDAR—1951 approximately 5½"x6¼"—Easel Type Desk Calendar. Two tone simulated embossed leather frame. Separate calendar card or page for every month, and on each one a new Esquire Girl picture in full color.
NO ADVERTISING MATTER OF ANY KIND APPEARS ANYWHERE ON THIS GIFT.

STRIKE!

WESTMINSTER SOCKS
SCORE WITH MEN

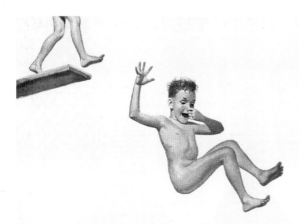

not a stitch in sight ...
on
the
new
Van Chick

In colors,
whites and stripes

Manhattan, 1952

a feast for the eyes!

What more could a man ask for! Just one touch of new, soft, smooth, Vanuana Sport Shirts and you'll be humming "Sweet Leilani" all season long. As luxurious and rich-looking as a tropical paradise . . . as cool and exciting as a night in Waikiki. Sixteen bright, solid, South Sea colors that dance before your eyes. Short sleeves. **$3.65** or long sleeves. **$4.50.**

Phillips-Jones Corp., N. Y. 1, N. Y., Makers of Van Heusen Shirts • Sport Shirts • Ties • Pajamas • Handkerchiefs • Collars

Van Heusen
REG. T. M.

Vanuana sport shirts

Van Heusen, 1951

for
swimming...

for
slimming...

there's
nothing
like
a Jantzen!

it's fabulous the way a Jantzen performs
on the body...the wonderful way it moulds
and smooths...the wonderful way it makes you look
and feel. There's nothing like it in the world...nothing
even remotely touches this dream for girls, the most
perfect swim suit ever made...finest nylon taffeta,
one-piece or two-piece 16.95...nothing like these
precision-tailored deluxe all-nylon boxers 4.95
...nothing like the fabulous new Jantzen colors.
Get yours...they're at most stores.

Matching Jantzen swim caps
and Jandals in stunning pastels

Jantzen

finest nylon
figuremaker
swim suits

Jantzen, 1951

everything a man ever wanted!

a brand new
look, cabana sets,
walking shorts, hot-weather shirts,
fast-drying nylon...everything with
famous Jantzen fit! See the cabana set,
far right, cool Sanforized cotton
Honolulu-here-we-come shirt 5.95,
boxer shorts 3.95...far left, Bermuda
walkers, British-cut, tailored like slacks,
in Sanforized cotton gabardine 5.95...
deluxe nylon boxer swim shorts and
marvelous "Nylastic" racers 4.95...
mesh tee shirts 2.95...all these and
more in the Jantzen line-up
...at most stores.

TAN with JAN
Oil or Lotion for a
glorious copper tan

Jantzen
Lastex-powered
swim trunks
sunclothes

torso-oh!

thanks
to **Jantzen**
"shapemakery"

"torso-oh" is any girl's torso under the influence of Jantzen "shapemakery", wonderful new figuremaking technique that transforms any girl into a bathing beauty complete with the new higher bustline, the new long-body look, the always glamorous slim waist and exciting curves. "Shapemakery" is an exclusive Jantzen feature, combines the best swim suit bras with the best torso control, on the job all the time. "On the dot" left and "fine line" right have marvelous Jantzen "stay-bras", come in ®Lastex-powered faille with ®Celaperm dots, dream colors 16.95.

Jantzen

most beautiful

most beautifying

swim suits in the world

Jantzen swim cap in heavenly Jantzen swim suit colors 1.50

Jantzen Inc · Portland 8 · Oregon

Jantzen, 1950 ◄

Jantzen, 1955

c'mon in ... the wearing's fine

Completely washable! They take to water like a mermaid. We're talking about
the new—and we mean *new!*—Van Gab sport shirts. *Gabardine*... like you've never
seen! *Silky-smooth gabardine*... with a new luxurious softness! *Finer-woven gabardine*
... that wears and wears and wears! We've tailored this fine fabric with
famous Van Heusen magic sewmanship. Full-cut for action ... figure-tapered for looks!
Shown here is famous California Lo-No model with exclusive two-way collar
... smart with or without a tie. Completely washable, stays size-right, color-fast. **$4.95**
See Van Gab gabardine in other smart models—$2.95 to $5.95

The ties: Van Heusen Washable Poplin in 100% Nylon, 18 solid-color Sportones...$1.50 each.
Phillips-Jones Corp., New York 1. Makers of Van Heusen Shirts • Ties • Pajamas • Collars • Sport Shirts

Van Heusen, 1950

Look at those collars again! California Lo-No with "Fadeaway Collarband". Looks, fits right . . . with or without tie.   Season's biggest splash of color with 21 bright, new washable "Aquashades

| Sunset Red | Sea Clay | Shell Pink | Mermaid Mauve | Mist Grey | Tropi-Tan | Dune Tan | Ocean Blue | Sky Blue | Billow Blue | Pirate Gold | Sand Tan | Beach Beige | Deep Green | Briny Green | Gulf Green | Spray Green | Turtle Green | Sunglow Yellow | Oyster | Foam White |

Van Heusen

REG. T. M.

new Van Gab Sport **Shirts** . . . *Completely washable* . . . $4.95

for
romancin'...

and
entrancin'

...there's nothing like a Jantzen!

for that matter there's nothing like a Jantzen for swimming
and slimming...nothing like the way a Jantzen fits, feels and
looks...nothing like the wonderful figure-making job a Jantzen
does...nothing like the marvelous Jantzen swim suit fabrics...
in particular, Jantzen Nylastic, the magic-moulding fast-drying
special Jantzen blend of nylon and laton, the finest swim
suit fabric ever made. Girl's suit, detailed for romance, with
marvelous Jantzen mouldable Stay-Bra 15.95...man's speed-cut
racers 5.95...terrific colors for everybody...at most stores.

Jantzen
Nylastic
nylon-with-laton
swim suits

Matching Jantzen swim caps
and Jondals in stunning pastels

J.C. Penny, 1956

...follow the sun—
and the open road...
in color-drenched cottons that do the most
wonderful things for your tan!...Ship'n Shore blouses
pack light, travel well—and keeping them
laundry-fresh is easy as a dip in the pool!
Upper left, 3.50...the others, **2.98**

get out...and get into a

Ship'n Shore®
blouse

Ship'n Shore

Ship'n Shore, 1953

The BEST in
BE-BOP GLASSES

ORIGINAL GENUINE

The STYLE sensation of the year.
You Don't Have To
"NEED" GLASSES to Wear BE-BOPS!
These glasses have no power.

DIES' GLITTER BE-BOP
autiful Lightweight ☐ Black
Brown or ☐ Blue Pearl ☐ Pink
arl frames. Gold decorated front
d sides. Clear White lens.
YLE No. 131
LADIES' STYLE..............Only **$3⁹⁵**
YLE No. 117
MEN'S SHAPE..................Only **$3⁹⁵**

sparkles Golden!

Bebop Glasses, 1950

Royal Crown, 1950

Nadinola, 1950

new shampoo sensation
actually <u>shines</u> hair

gets it so clean you can feel the difference!

Now bring out the *full* beauty of your hair with a revolutionary shampoo that works in a completely new way! Helene Curtis Shampoo Whip bombards hair and scalp with billions of lively, lanolin-loaded bubbles that *rush* dirt and dandruff away—even in hardest water. Leaves it so gloriously fresh and clean you can *feel* the difference. So sunbeam bright...so enchantingly soft...you'll take new, exciting pride in your hair.

It's the world's first whipped LOTION-LATHER shampoo—wonderfully *good* for your hair and scalp. A marvelous beauty treat—with amazing new *atomized* lanolin, that penetrates like magic mist to EVERY part of hair and scalp. MORE lanolin by far than ordinary shampoos.

And because of miraculous LOTION-LATHER, *this* shampoo leaves hair easier to manage than ever before. NO drying, oil-robbing action to leave hair strawlike, unruly. Helene Curtis Shampoo Whip gives hair rich glowing beauty never before possible without costly special after-rinse.

This amazing new discovery by Helene Curtis, leading authority on hair, makes ordinary shampoos old-fashioned. Try it today, and you will throw away your *old* shampoos.

Just press nozzle ——→
and out billows rich
ACTUAL LATHER
(like whipped cream)

Helene Curtis
SHAMPOO
WHIP

Not a Soap, Creme or Liquid but a revolutionary new Helene Curtis discovery—the World's first whipped LOTION-LATHER shampoo!

SO ECONOMICAL !
HALF-YEAR SUPPLY... $1

New! Bombards dirt and dandruff with billions of microscopic bubbles!

Gets hair so clean you can feel the difference.

New! Guaranteed—far more applications for one dollar than any previous shampoo!

Wonderful for the WHOLE family!

New! Atomized-lanolin gets hair fabulously soft, magically obedient!

Far MORE lanolin than any ordinary shampoo.

Helene Curtis, 1950

The newer, nicer kind of bathroom tissue

Soft-Weve belongs in the well-appointed bathroom

Gentle as facial tissue... two soft thicknesses—firm and strong

In the well-appointed bathrooms of today you almost always find this new facial-soft tissue—Soft-Weve.

Soft-Weve is the newer, nicer kind of bathroom tissue. It's two thicknesses soft—two thicknesses strong and firm. For *your* home, your family and your guests—be sure to provide facial-soft Soft-Weve. It's the up-to-date bathroom tissue. And it's another great Scott paper value . . . every modern home can enjoy it.   "SOFT-WEVE", REG. U. S. PAT. OFF.

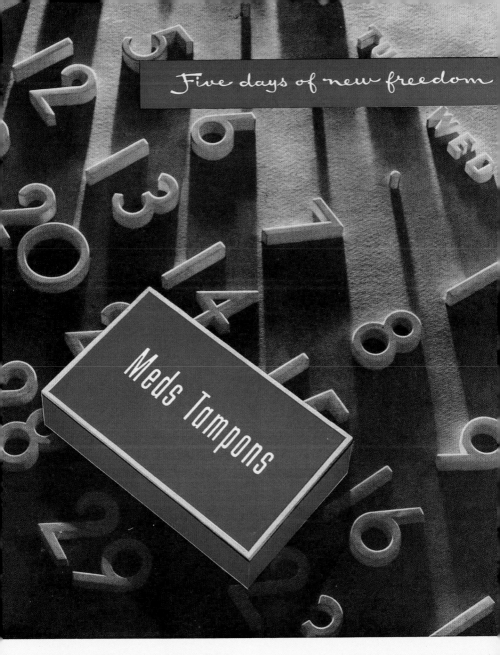

Five days of new freedom

Meds Tampons

YOUR FIRST PACKAGE
FREE!

We know that once you try Meds®—the safer, softer tampon—and discover those five days of new freedom every month, you'll be a Meds tampon user ever after! Mail us the back panel from the first Meds box of 10 you buy, with your name and address. We'll return the full price—39¢. Personal Products Corp., Dept. D-7, Milltown, N.J. (Offer expires Oct. 31, 1954.)

I dreamed
I had Spring Fever

in my
maidenform bra

For the figure of your fondest day-dreams—Maidenform's lovely new Concerto* gives you curves that are more
curvaceous, brings an exciting line to your outline! And it's all accomplished with row
upon row of tiny, interlocked stitches! Each stitch catches up an inner cup-lining, pre-shapes this bra *just* enough
to mould a fabulous form! In white stitched broadcloth, lace-margined. AA, A, B and C sizes...2.00

*REG U. S. PAT. OFF.   ©1956 MAIDEN FORM BRASSIERE CO., INC.

Maidenform, 1956

Maidenform, 1954

the genius of Peter Pan shapes a beautiful future!

PETER PAN

There's a more exciting summer in store for you! Choose the Peter Pan strapless bra made to make you look your loveliest in all your bare-shoulder fashions:

FREEDOM RING† (*left*), a new revolutionary *wired* bra that brings you peace of mind—unique spring action takes all irritating pressure off sensitive areas. Comes with Hidden Treasure or Inner Circle cup.

INNER CIRCLE* (*center*), for the average or full-average bust. The exclusive Dura-form cup guarantees uplift that *keeps up* for the long life of the bra.

HIDDEN TREASURE* (*right*), the most famous bra in the world, for the small bust or in-between size. The patented Magicup adds fullness *confidentially*, without pads or puffs.

PETER PAN FOUNDATIONS, INC.

FIFTH AVENUE, NEW YORK

MERRY-GO-ROUND OF CANADA, MONTREAL, QUEBEC

Peter Pan, 1954

► *Hollywood Maxwell Company, 1951*

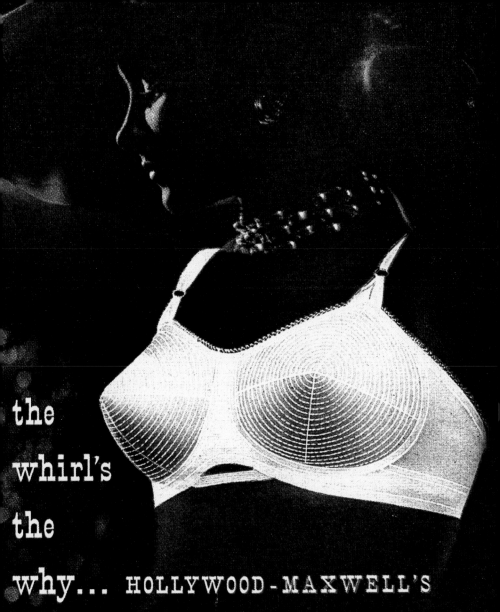

the

whirl's

the

why... HOLLYWOOD-MAXWELL'S

V-ETTE *Whirlpool* BRAS*

IT'S A BLOUSE...IT'S A SLIP...ALL IN ONE!

Blue Swan Slipmates

SCHOOL | SPORTS

HOME | WORK

$2.98

SIZES 32 (dress 9/10) to 40 (dress 17/18)
Also TEEN SIZES for ages 10-12-14

- **ECONOMICAL** . . . Serves a Double Purpose!
- **FASHIONABLE** . . . Styled For Wear Almost Everywhere!
- **NEAT** . . . The Blouse Can't Slip Out!
- **SMOOTH-FITTING** . . . Cut From Exacting Slip Patterns!
- **PRACTICAL** . . . As Easy To Wash As a Regular Slip!

Just slip into Slipmates — step into a skirt and you're smartly dressed! Wonderful for wear with a suit too! The blouse top is styled with the popular "bat" sleeves in soft interlock combed cotton jersey with a smart heather effect. Permanently attached is a runproof tricot rayon half slip that beautifully molds to your figure. A clever new idea — at an unbelievably low price.

Hurry to your favorite store for your Slipmates today!

JUST ADD A SKIRT

CREATORS OF
Suspants and **minikins**

Blouse tops in a choice of lovely heather tones.
GOLDEN ERA YELLOW • DRAMATIC RED • FLIGHT BLUE • GLAMOUR PINK
DYNAMIC GREEN • AUTUMN RUST • FROSTY WHITE

Available at Knit Lingerie Departments and Specialty Shops or write
BLUE SWAN MILLS, DIV. OF McKAY PRODUCTS CORP., 350 FIFTH AVE., N. Y., N. Y.

McKay Products Corporation, 1950

Exquisite Form Brassieres, 1950

Frederick's of Hollywood, 1951

Glamorous Lingerie

SHE'LL TREASURE WITH PLEASURE

"Day-Of-The-Week" BRAS

7 LOVABLE rayon satin bras, with contrasting net heart embroidered with the "Day-of-the-Week." Famous for firm uplift, fine separation. Adjustable shoulder straps for perfect comfort. In 7 Lovable colors to match colors of panties.

SIZES:
A Cups — 32, 34, 36.
B Cups — 32, 34, 36, 38.

7 for $6.99
BEAUTIFULLY GIFT BOXED

"Day-Of-The-Week" PANTIES

7 Hollywood Brief panties — made of resist-run rayon Tricot Jersey . . . embroidered with the "Day-of-the-Week." In 7 lovable colors to match colors of bras. Elastic waistband. Colorfast. Sizes: Small, Medium, Large. Styled by PLYMOUTH.

7 for $4.99
BEAUTIFULLY GIFT BOXED

BRA and PANTY COLORS
- Monday Blue
- Tuesday Pink
- Wednesday White
- Thursday Maize
- Friday Pink
- Saturday Black
- Sunday White

FITTED NEGLIGEE and GOWN SET

Thrillingly sheer rayon-ninon extravagantly combined with Chantilly lace. Gown has an all lace bodice,—negligee has an enchanting lace collar and fitted lace midriff. Push-up sleeves with dainty lace ruffles. Gorgeously transparent . . . (they wash like a dream . . . will not shrink!) Colors: Midnight Black, Pink Angel, Forget-me-not Blue, Bridal White. Sizes: 12 to 18.

2 PIECE SET $12.99
GIFT BOXED

Styled by MURRAY OLIPHANT

DUSTER-ROBE, PAJAMA and SCUFF SET

Elegant duster-robe has full swinging back, belts three ways with its own self-sash! Quilted wing collar and cuffs. Multi-color floral appliqué on pockets. 2-piece pajamas have gayly contrasting piping and buttons in a pretty Mandarin style that's tops in comfort! Complete set made of petal-soft, doeskin-finish French rayon crepe that's washable, quick-drying! Matching quilted scuffs, with dainty ruching, have waterproof plastic soles. Colors: American Beauty, Aqua, or Royal Blue. Sizes: 9 to 17 and 10 to 18.

4 PIECE SET $8.99
GIFT BOXED

Styled by PEGGY PRIM

EXOTIC MANDARIN LOUNGING and SLEEPING PAJAMAS

The Mandarin jacket has all sorts of authentic details . . . real frog closings, side slits, a tiny high collar. And just for a touch of elegance, the big patch pocket is appliquéd with a Navy Blue Chinese dragon. So light and comfortable she'll sleep in them, too! Made of wonderfully practical seersucker (suds in a jiffy . . . never needs ironing!). Jacket in choice of: Coral, Maize, Robins Egg Blue. Navy Blue trousers only. Sizes: 10-20; 9-19.

2 PIECE SET $5.99
Gift Boxed

WHAT LOVELY GIFTS! Order by Mail!

Jonas Shoppes
Dept. L-745
6th Ave. at 14th St., N. Y. 11

Please send me the following items.
Add 31c to each item for postage and handling.

Item	Quantity	Size	Color	2nd Color Choice
Boxed Bra Set at $6.99			7 lovable colors	
Boxed Panty Set at $4.99			7 lovable colors	
Negligee & Gown Set at $12.99				
Duster-Robe, Pajama and Scuff Set $8.99				
Lounging and Sleeping Pajamas at $5.99				

NAME ....

ADDRESS ....

CITY .... ZONE .... STATE ....

Save C.O.D. Charges by sending check or money order.

☐ Money Order ☐ Check ☐ C.O.D.
(If delivered in New York City, add 3% Sales Tax) MONEY BACK GUARANTEE WITHIN 5 DAYS

FREE! 16 PAGE GIFT CATALOG. WRITE FOR YOUR COPY TODAY.

Jonas Shoppes, 1952

None

So

Cool

These are the panties that never get clingy, never feel clammy—even on the warmest days. Cool in Summer, comfortable always, because they're naturally absorbent!

the **KNIT**
with the **FIT**
where you **SIT**

They g-i-v-e with every motion, really fit your figure— they're made for an active life. Easy to care for, they wash and dry quickly, need no ironing. All panty styles.

PANTIES OF

®*Spun-lo*

RAYON FABRIC

ONLY ABOUT **69¢**

Perma·lift
GIRDLES
NO BONES ABOUT IT
STAYS UP WITHOUT STAYS

ONLY

PERMA·LIFT girdles

have the Magic Inset

No Bones About It—

Stays Up Without Stays

Whether you're on a social spree or a workaday whirl, you're the picture of fashion with a new "Perma·lift"* Girdle. Here's the brightest, lightest, smartest, smoothest girdle you ever wore and oh! so comfortable. Not a bone or stay to poke or pinch—just the lasting stay-up smartness of the Magic Inset delicately designed in the front panel. Your dainty "Perma·lift" Girdle can't roll over, wrinkle or bind—it stays up without stays. Select the style just right for you at your favorite corset department—$5.00 to $10.95.

Also enjoy a "Perma-lift" Bra—America's best loved bra with "The Lift that never lets you down."

·"Perma-lift" a trade-mark of A. Stein & Company (Reg. U. S. Pat. Off.)

Look for th
Magic Ins

Industrial Rayon Corporation, 1954

Perma-lift Girdles, 1950

With a Flair for casual smartness

Want comfort? Want good looks, too? Get yourself an Arrow Dude Ranch sport shirt. This collection includes beautifully tailored neat checks and plaids. It features the regular-length sports shirt collar, or new short points. (The collars on *all* Arrow sports shirts have the new *Arafold* construction that makes them look, fit, feel better.) Fabrics are colorfast, "Sanforized" ® cottons. $5.95. Why not pick out a few now. Cluett, Peabody & Co., Inc.

Arrow dude ranch

Another smartly styled **ARROW SPORTS SHIRT**

DIAMOND HEAD MOUNTAIN IN BACKGROUND

Handsome new tropical color...it's the **DOBBS** *Hawaii Tan*

Ride the crest of the new color fashion wave in straw hats —
Hawaii Tan. Here's a rich, deep tropical tan,
an original shade created by Dobbs. Note the new Diamond Head
soft roll crown, and the exclusive black-gold band...
superb details of Dobbs styling. $10.

*Other Dobbs Straw Hats from $5.00 to $100.
At the finer stores.*

DOBBS HATS, NEW YORK'S LEADING HATTER, PARK AVENUE AT THE WALDORF, NEW YORK 22, N. Y.
ESQUIRE : *June*

Dobbs Hats, 1953

KNOX

Straw Hats of Distinction

$5.00 to $20.00

Featuring an outstanding collection
of exclusive, colorful bands.

KNOX

Knox, 1953

new school of design in ties

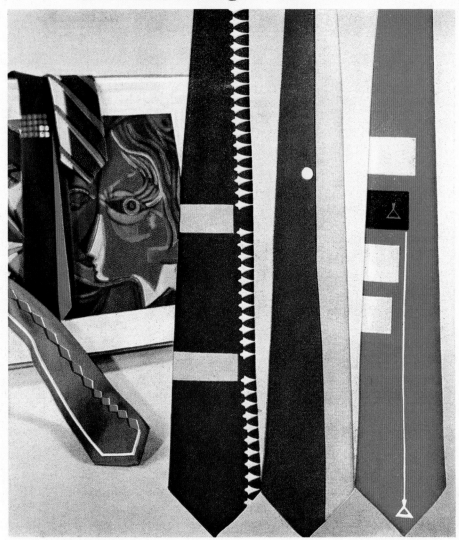

"side glances"

Manhattan combines the conservative and the unusual in a refreshing new note in printed acetate foulard neckwear. These new "Side Glance" ties offer distinctive designs—with the focus of interest on one side of the tie! In a wide array of color combinations—from bright to subdued.

styled by

**SIDE GLANCES NECKWEAR, $1.50
OTHERS TO $3.50**

© 1953, THE MANHATTAN SHIRT CO., 444 MADISON AVENUE, NEW YORK, N. Y.

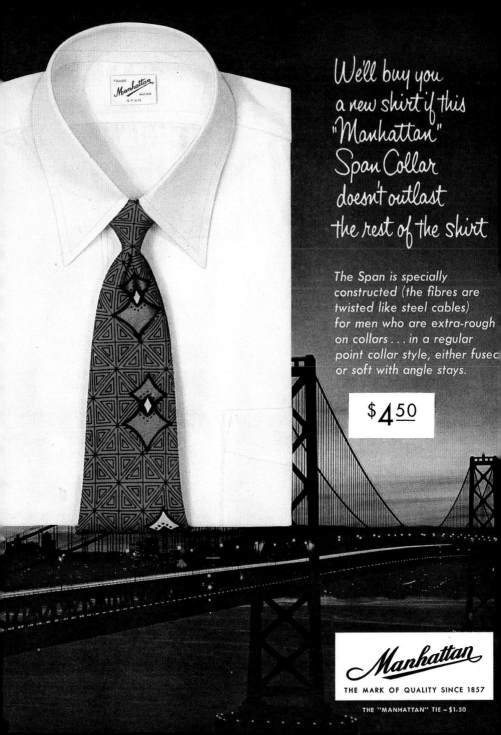

We'll buy you a new shirt if this "Manhattan" Span Collar doesn't outlast the rest of the shirt

The Span is specially constructed (the fibres are twisted like steel cables) for men who are extra-rough on collars... in a regular point collar style, either fused or soft with angle stays.

$4⁵⁰

Manhattan

THE MARK OF QUALITY SINCE 1857

THE "MANHATTAN" TIE — $1.50

Smartly Tailored
for Smart Relaxing

Look as good as you *feel* in your "easy-time" clothes!

These distinguished new Arrow Sports Shirts were made to give you casual comfort with the smartest style this side of Bikini. Tailored of a premium all-rayon fabric that's color-fast *and* WASHABLE, these eye-catching prints come in more color combinations, than you can shake a palm leaf at!

Short sleeves, $5. Some with long sleeves, $5.95. Cluett, Peabody & Co., Inc.

Arrow
Caribbean
Prints

take a leaf from
Jinx's book and put your clan
in McGregor tartans!

Make your Dad
Very
Important
Pop
of the year!

Give Dad a gift
by McGregor...
with a card **you** sign
in gold naming Pop
V.I.P. of the year!

Sure—Dad's important the year
'round! But you can tell him how
very important he is on Father's
Day in a way he'll treasure all his
life . . . on a card *you* sign in gold.
Enclose it with the Gift of the Year:
The McGregor Flamingo Holiday
Set. Of washable cotton Madras,
the shirt has new freedom sleeve.
Linen-like Scotlin slacks are of rayon and nylon. Set with belt—15.95

The Shirt, 5.95
The Slacks, 10.95

Good News for Mom! All McGregor
V.I.P. Shirts are washable. And
McGregor Flamingo outfits just like
Dad's are boy-sized, boy-priced, too!

Swim Set of the Year—
Biscayne—colorfully
matching patterned shirts and
shorts. Shirt 7.95. Shorts 5.95

Wash-whiz of the
Year! Linen-like Scotlin
shirts. Richly hued rayon.
Avcomet finish. 5.00 S.S.
Won't shrink or fade ever.

Fancy Shirt of the
Year. "Sheer Madness."
Cool Madras. 5.95

Big Wheel of the Year.
"Wagon Wheels"! Cool, full
cut, spread collar, short
sleeve shirt. 5.00

Mesh Shirt of the Year!
Icy-cool Arctic Ayre has
smart 2-way collar. 5.95

McGREGOR*
Sportswear

MADE
IN
U.S.A.

DAVID D. DONIGER & CO., INC., 373 FIFTH AVENUE, NEW YORK 16, N.Y. *TRADE MARK

Carter's, 1950

► Carter's, 1956

Little Yankee, 1953

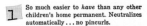
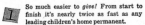
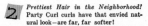

119

Lilt, 1954

BILTWEL

HONEYLANE

KERRYBROOKE

Off to a flying start...in new

NEW CORDUROY CREATIONS FOR GIRLS!

A. The full-circle sweep of this new Honeylane skirt is even more dramatic in fall's newest color, star sapphire blue. The skirt, in washable fine wale corduroy, also comes in sophisticated black and favorite bright red. Plastic patent belt. Sizes 7-14, **3.49**

Smart companion is the sissy front white cotton broadcloth blouse with pert johnny collar and tie. Front has 6 rows of crisp nylon acetate lace, with ruffly lace on sleeves. Washable. Sizes 7-14, **2.49**

B. After-school fun calls for a Honeylane car-coat jacket with toggle buttons, self-hook closings, Ivy-style patch pockets and a cozy collar that converts to a hood!

Matching Italian style pants (note new length) have tapered legs, Ivy-style adjustable buckle back, band top and zipper fly front...a mannish side pocket, too! Both coat and pants are Sears fine wale washable corduroy. Mix or match 'em in star sapphire blue, red, or black. Sizes 7-14. Jacket, **4.98** Pants, **2.98**

C. Honeylane "Dutch Boy" suspender skirt can be worn with or without suspenders. Pegged skirt has soft, unpressed pleats. Washable, fine wale corduroy. Star sapphire blue, black, and red. Sizes 7-14, **3.98**

Cuddly Honeylane pullover in washable Orlon* has the mock-turtle neck that's making sweater-set news.. plus special stitching to give a full fashioned look. Rib knit neck, cuffs and bottom band. Yellow, white, black, red, turquoise. Sizes 7-14, **3.49**

Mix 'em, Match 'em! Wash 'em, Dry 'em! All girls' styles are designed so that any part of one ensemble will go with any other. Here, in three low-cost ensembles, is a complete school wardrobe...and it's all fully washable, carefree as clothes can be!

4 easy ways to buy school clothes at Sears—Purchases of $20 or more can be made on Sears Easy Payment Plan. Sears stores feature the Lay-Away Plan, or Credit Purchase Coupon Books you can use like cash. Many stores offer Sears Revolving Charge Accounts, too.

Biltwel Ivy-style saddle with smart strap and buckle in back. White with real brown, or black. **3.98**

"Toggle" shoe worn with strap up or swiveled down as a pump. Striped lining. Black, red, black patent. **4.98**

Classic Biltwel slip-on moc has long-wearing Searolite sole. Red, brown or black. Kerrybrooke teen sizes, too. **5.98**

Sears, 1951

Sears own exclusive brands are styled with authority:

BILTWEL · HONEYLANE
KERRYBROOKE · FRATERNITY PREP
GOLD BOND · BOYVILLE

Guaranteed and sold only by Sears

school styles from Sears!

CLASSIC IVY LOOK STYLES FOR BOYS!

D. The big fellow wears Fraternity Prep Ivy-style trousers in all-wool flannel, with classic back belt, no pleats, tapered legs. Cambridge gray or charcoal gray, stripe or solid. Waist sizes 26-31, **6.98**

Classic Ivy-style dress shirt in Sanforized, combed cotton oxford cloth has button-down collar, back button and box-pleated back. Sizes 6-20, white or blue, **2.49**

Handsome Fraternity Prep sweater is washable, high-bulk virgin Orlon*. In 5 colors, **3.98**

*DuPont acrylic fiber

E. Ivy-style Fraternity Prep trousers in sturdy, 9-oz. polished cotton are machine-washable, need little or no ironing. Pleatless, back-belt style. Mercerized, Sanforized. Beige or black. Sizes 8-20, **3.98**

The very correct long-sleeve Ivy sport shirt has button-down collar. *Perma-Smooth* finish on yarn-dyed combed cotton requires little or no ironing. In stripes of red, brown, or blue. Sizes 10-20, **2.49** Ivy-style, polished cotton cap to match trousers, **1.69**

F. Big style for little fellows! Boyville trousers of exclusive Searalon (rayon and acetate, 21% nylon sheen gabardine) are crease resistant, spot resistant and water repellent. Matching belt included. In skipper blue, charcoal, dark brown. Sizes 4-10, **3.98**

Ivy stripes distinguish new Boyville short-sleeve sport shirt with button-down collar. Knit from combed cotton yarns for easy washability. Handsome assortment of styles and colors. Sizes 4-10, **1.79**

Shop at Sears and save

You'll enjoy shopping at Sears Stores and Sears Catalog Sales Offices. It's convenient to shop from the Sears Catalog in your home, too, by mail or phone. Sears employes, you know, are the largest owners of the Sears business. They'll do their best to serve you well

SATISFACTION GUARANTEED OR YOUR MONEY BACK

SEARS ROEBUCK AND CO.

"Look, Mom, no laces! Boys' Biltwel with Shu-Lok® flips open, closed. Soles guaranteed 4 months. Black, brown. **7.98**

Carefree, yet correct. Boys' Gold Bond Jelly Roll slip-on in long-wearing, polished black or brown leather. **5.98**

Top grain leather. Brand new Biltwel "football toe." Searolite sole for long wear. Black or brown. **5.50**

You're the Casual Type in Keds

You feel a different guy the minute your feet sink into a pair of Casual Keds. Here's quiet, cushion-y luxury that offers a life of ease all day. Your feet are on an air-cooled vacation in these summery shoes that breathe when you walk. And they come in so many handsome styles and colors— all washable—you can wear Keds everywhere!

BOOSTERS
Brown, Blue, Natural.
Faded Blue Denim, Maine Brown
Maize, Green, Claret.

BAREFOOT SANDALS
Team these with shorts, or slacks.
Instep straps woven with
Lastex. Maize, Claret.

DENIM SLIP-ONS
Instep gores made with Lastex
cling yet never bind.
Brown or Faded Blue Denim.

LOOP-TIES
Town smoothies, are right at home
in the country, too.
Maine Brown, Blue, Green.

GORE CASUALS
Just slip them on—
they're eased with Lastex.
Maine Brown or Blue.

CLEAT-TRED OXFORDS
Slipproof soles for campus or golf.
Maine Brown, Sand.

u.s. Keds
The Shoes of Champions—They Wash

UNITED STATES RUBBER COMPANY
Rockefeller Center, New York

Style #9291
Classic Summer style.
Dressy wing tip with
flexible leather sole.

Style #9759
Smart ventilated styl[e]
Moccasin toe for ext[ra]
foot freedom. Fi[ne]
leather sole.

Style #9610
Genuine Nylon Mesh
inlay. Flexible leather
sole. Feather-light and
wonderfully cool.

Freshen up...
FROM THE GROUND UP...IN
America's No.1 Shoe

Thom McAn's prices for style-right, summer-right shoe values are so
down-to-earth that you *can* afford to stride through any summer scene looking and feeling like a cool,
cool million! There's a reason for Thom McAn's sensible prices: Thom McAn is America's
largest manufacturer-retailer of men's shoes. Huge production brought directly to
you through Thom McAn's own retail stores, means big savings which are passed along to *you*.
No wonder so many men are buying two pairs of Thom McAns—for less money
than they previously spent for only one pair of high-priced shoes.

See them—try them—and you, too, will say:

"I don't see how they make them for the money."

Thom McAn
WORN BY MORE MEN THAN ANY OTHER SHOE

$7⁹⁵ AND
$8⁹⁵
MOST STYLES

The Fall American Look

It's a look of unwrinkled neatness and casual comfort

e-x-p-a-n-d-s

ONE SIZE FITS ALL

EXCLUSIVE WITH
ESQUIRE SOCKS
"The smartest thing on two feet"

ORDINARY SOCKS look like this

e-x-p-a-n-d-s socks fit like this . . . f.rever, because only e-x-p-a-n-d-s all-nylon socks fit as though custom-knit for you alone.

"10-2-14" RIB — The original e-x-p a-n-d-s rib in a year-round weight.
"SENATOR" — Specially patterned clock in flat knit e-x-p-a-n-d-s.
"VEEP" — Heavier gauge link 'n link design e-x-p-a-n-d-s.

Individually Gift Boxed
The perfect gift . . . guaranteed for one year against holes caused by wear.

Walk-Over
Broadmoor Brogue
No. 3490

THE FALL

DIV OF CHESTER H. ROTH CO., INC.

Stetson, 1954

They'll Sweep You off Your Feet!

Step into a pair of colorful Commodores, to enjoy all the carefree comfort that BALL-BAND builds into lightweight casuals. Look forward to enjoying your Commodores for a long time for they are of BALL-BAND Quality, with scrubbable fabric uppers *vulcanized* to rubber soles. Buoyant Duo-Texture platforms with genuine rubber bindings. Ask for Commodores with the famous Red Ball trade-mark.

TRADE
MARK

NAVY BLUE   MAPLE BROWN   FADED BLUE   MAIZE   RED   BROWN   NATURAL   WINE   GREEN

MEN'S AND WOMEN'S   .   WOMEN'S   MEN'S

COMMODORES
by BALL-BAND
MISHAWAKA · INDIANA

Fine fitting Dura-Duk uppers
for cool comfort. Springy crepe
rubber soles and bindings are
vulcanized on to stay.

Scrubbable denim or twill uppers in an array of smart shades.
Vulcanized cork-lightened rubber soles, genuine rubber bindings.

Ball-Band, 1952

Neither value nor economy
depends necessarily on how much
you spend, but rather on what
you get! Florsheim Shoes are made
to look better and to last longer...
so that you spend less in the long
run for the finest shoes it's possible
to make. Figure your shoe costs
by the month and by the mile,
and you'll choose Florsheims!

The KENMOOR, S-1401,
popular U-wing tip style.

The Florsheim Shoe Company
Chicago 6 · Makers of Fine Shoes
for Men and Women

Florsheim
quality

Florsheim, 1957

It's feather-light yet rugged . . .
dries in minutes! Yes, Du Pont nylon
makes you *look* good out of the water,
feel good in. And you'll find swimwear of
Du Pont nylon in the very
latest, smartest styles.

Man's idea of a
rugged swimsuit...
Du Pont Nylon

DU PONT
REG. U. S. PAT. OFF.

BETTER THINGS FOR BETTER LIVING...*THROUGH CHEMISTRY*

new things are happening in **NYLON**—one of **DU PONT'S** modern-living

☎ *Call Western Union by number in the cities listed on page 149
and ask for Operator 25 to learn where to buy this merchandise*

Du Pont, 1955

★ Jantzen has the walkers...perfect-fitting walkers...
tailored like slacks...with five waistband styles
...five lengths from four inches to ten inches...
fourteen of the finest fabrics...sixteen good-looking
colors...the biggest, best parade of walkers in
America. "Dacrolin golfer", famous Jantzen zip-fit
waistband, eight-inch, linen-and-Dacron blend, has
towel and tee tabs 7.95..."off duty tens", super
burley 7.95..."flannel walker", eight-inch, rayon
flannel 7.95..."clansman walker", eight-inch,
imported English gingham, authentic clan plaid 7.95
..."chino walkers", six-inch, chino twill 4.95.

★ Striped shirt 4.95...others 3.95...
all finest-quality cotton.

★ Men's walker socks by Jantzen 1.50.

Jantzen ®

is the
walker champion!

flannel
eights 7.95

off-duty
tens 7.95

clansman
eights 7.95

chino
sixes 4.95

*Call Western Union by number in the cities listed on page 149
and ask for Operator 25 to learn where to buy this merchandise*

Jantzen, 1955

A Special Father's Day Gift Tag,
with space for your signature, is looped
to each of the soft, super-smooth Marlboro
Jerdange sport shirt classics illustrated above.
They're Marlboro's exclusive, eye-filling Paddock
Patterns, inspired by America's smartest
tracks and luxury resorts.

BECAUSE YOUR
HEART BELONGS
TO DADDY

Marlboro
Parades to the Post
(For Father's Day — June 18th)

A Special Father's Day Gift Box is your
presentation package for these front-row, cucumber-cool favorites:
A — Frankona, B — Sta-Cool, C — Ventelator. You'll find
them, and D — Sta-Cool Dress Shirt, E — Skygab Soap 'n Water and
F — Summer Cool Dress Shirt, in 25 out-of-this-world Turf Tones
that make them odds-on Father's Day favorites.

1950's SPORT SHIRT CLASSICS

Marlboro Shirt Company, 1950

BRIGHT FUTURE

all because of no-fade Coloray* these **B.V.D.**" sport shirts will stay bright!

HANDSOME? You bet. Clean-cut patterns in clean-tailored shirts with ease sewn in from collar to cuff. The colors are clear but not loud . . . combinations of brights and grays. Very smart from November to November! And because they're Coloray colors, they'll never fade out or cloud over. The rayon fabric by Burlington feels like worsted . . . washes like crazy. Regular sizes, $5. At all good stores, or write Courtaulds (Alabama) Inc., 600 Fifth Ave., N. Y. 20.

Coloray, 1957

A nimated S tyle

Spring wears her heart on your sleeve when you take your pick from these wondrous fabrics. Rarely was there a match like this—the fire of Animated Style wedded to the mellowness of fine spun cloth. If you have a flair for fashion, Hammonton Park Clothes will bring a light to your eyes. Strike up an acquaintance now with the store in town displaying the famous Style Trophy.

HAMMONTON PARK CLOTHES
Dept. E-54, 200 Fifth Avenue, New York 10, N. Y.

This trophy has been awarded to selected stores that have attained and maintained style eminence.

Hammonton Park Clothes, 1950

Authentic D. & J. Anderson Plaid with unusual Buckle $2.50

Imported Blocked Wool Challis $2.50

D. & J. Anderson Authentic Tartan Plaid $2.50

Imported India Madras Stripes $2.50

The Ivy Influence BY PARIS

If you saw your belt as others see it, you'd change it more often

If your belt is worn and old fashioned, select one of Paris'* brightest styles. Smart new designs closely following the Ivy Influence are extremely popular and, of course, made in the traditional high Paris quality.

PARIS BELTS • SUSPENDERS • GARTERS

Reg. U.S. Pat. Off. · A product of A. Stein & Company · Chicago · New York · Los Angeles

A. Stein & Company, 1957

you're a "man alive" in a CLIPPER CRAFT suit

$50 to $60

Best-rated attraction in town — that's you in a Clipper Craft suit or sportcoat. That man-of-action styling,
those lively yet dignified patterns make the prettiest heads turn ... the toughest critics rave!
In long shots or close-ups you're the star in their eyes ... because Clipper Craft's
virile tailoring ... the rugged, yet sophisticated good looks of the masterful suit you're wearing
tell the world you're a man in the know! You'll say "Man Alive!" to the low price too,
because Clipper Craft combines the purchasing power of 1226 stores to keep you best dressed for less.

For the store nearest you, write: Dept. E117 CLIPPER CRAFT, 18 Station Street, Boston 20, Massachusetts.

CLIPPER CRAFT CLOTHES

127

Clipper Craft, 1957

Eagle Clothes, 1951 ▶▶ *Daroff, 1955*

Paint your own picture
of a color-right wardrobe with

'BOTANY

TOWN BROWN

New shades of brown for in-town or *out-of-town*, for smart dress-up occasions or relaxed informal liv Above is the luxurious 2-ply 100% virgin worsted in rich new TOWN BROWN shade.

BLACK COFFEE

The addition of black to brown shades creates stimulating rich color effects—strong, masculine—every one a *bracer* for your wardrobe. Illustrated: the 100% virgin wool flannel suit in the new BLACK COFFEE.

'500'*
tailored by
DAROFF

From our "Gallery of Fashion"—

the **best** colors for

the **wardrobe** needs of

America's best-dressed men

from $65

PRICES SLIGHTLY HIGHER IN THE WEST.

SMOKE GREYS

Greys as you like them, in a variety of soft, muted shade —the tones that are more flattering to more men. Here you see SMOKE GREY in the new Hairline Worsted suit of 100% virgin worsted.

INK BLUES

The indispensable blue suits—blue in *any* hue, ranging all the way from the ultra-smart blackened midnight tones to the brighter, lighter chalky shades. As shown, INK BLUE in the luxurious 100% virgin worsted Sheen Gabardine Suit.

"Dress right—you can't afford not to"

Clans on Parade

Van Heusen calls the clans together to achieve the most original array of sport shirts *any* side of Edinburgh. This collection of 24 new Clanarama sport shirts starts with three vibrant classic tartans—then takes off from there with these new and exciting adaptations in stripes and checks. Rich, glowing and exceptionally clear, they have a Scottish flavor all their own. In a new and specially constructed Dan River cotton woven exclusively for Van Heusen. Completely washable and only **$5.00.**

New Clanarama Stripes and Checks by

VAN HEUSEN

Enro Shirt Company, 1958

▶ *Marlboro Shirt Company, 1954*

reading, riting 'n romance

Exciting new **COLLEGE** and **CAREER** fashions to please that favorite sweetheart. Marlboro handles color like an M.A.— comes up with rich, warm fabric and fashion ideas. **NO DOUBT ABOUT THIS DATE.**

from the

Marlboro
album of sportswear

THE "DRAKE"
Warm, rich, new styled smartness goes everywhere. Washable blend 60% wool and 40% rayon.

7.95

BIG TIMBER "VERONA"
Confined originals in fabric and style. Fully Washable cotton.

4.95

"FIESTA PLAIDS"
Confined originals—warm to feel, warm to color—worn to every occasion. Avcoset finished rayon for permanent rayon washability. 7.95

RINKLE SHAKER "FRONTIER" EMBLEM
Fly-Front embroidered magic—Cloud Mist colors in fully washable cotton. 5.95

"PAGEANTRY IN COLOR"
Magnificent space patterned colorings. Cleverly styled in panel front effects. Fully washable viscose.

4.95

MELLOROY "BEAUCOUP"
Plenty and pleasurable to live in all season. Three way cotton knit trim on corduroy comfort. Washable.

6.95

Marlboro SHIRT CO., INC., BALTIMORE 1, MD.
NEW YORK — Empire State Bldg. • LOS ANGELES — Wm. Fox Bld
CHICAGO

new PANAGRA COTTONS
by EVERFAST*
in brilliant

Fly PANAGRA to glorious South America today . . . wear your Panagra Cottons there tomorrow! It's the fastest U. S. Commercial Airline . . . winner of the coveted Frye Speed Trophy . . . and the world's friendliest! Leave any day via Panagra . . . board *El InterAmericano*, the luxurious express sleeper, at Miami and enjoy red carpet service all the way. Remember, Panagra is the *only* U. S. airline with twenty-four years' experience flying South America's West Coast. See your Travel Agent or any office of Pan American Airways (*U. S. General Sales Agents*).

PANAGRA
PAN AMERICAN-GRACE AIRWAYS

Everfast Fabrics, 1953

Panagra *El Inter Americano*

South American colors

COLE of California chose this striking striped Panagra Cotton by EVERFAST for a stunning swim suit. It is just one of an exciting collection of stripes and prints—all vibrant with color, authentic in concept—taking their theme from the rich lore and vivid beauty of South America—just a sky away via Panagra. Everfast designers borrowed colors and ideas from Argentina, Bolivia, Chile and Peru ...blending all together in a thrilling group of new fabrics.

Suit by COLE *of California in a Panagra Cotton by Everfast, made crease-resistant by Everglaze. Sizes Small, Medium and Large, about $15 at*
BONWIT TELLER, NEW YORK, CARSON, PIRIE SCOTT and Co., *Chicago,* NEIMAN-MARCUS CO., *Dallas,* SCRUGGS-VANDERVOORT-BARNEY, *St. Louis,* CITY OF PARIS DRY GOODS CO., *San Francisco, and leading stores everywhere.*

COLORS GUARANTEED BY EVERFAST FABRICS inc.

Reg. U. S. Pat. Off

Style 124, high-waisted Sarong of light nylon power net and embroidered nylon marquisette. White, black or pink. Sizes 25 to 34. $13.50. Other styles from $7.95.

she's wearing a **sarong**®

the criss-cross girdle that walks and won't ride up

Sarong is completely different from any other girdle — and you'll feel the difference immediately!
There is nothing like a Sarong to fashion your figure with new shapeliness, to make comfort
your personal and permanent possession. Sarong is so wonderfully different!!
Its patented, hidden construction lifts and flattens your tummy youthfully. Its exclusive
patented criss-cross feature lets you walk, stand and sit with day-long comfort.
From the moment you slip it on — you'll see and feel your figure improve.
Why not plan to have a Sarong fitted to your figure.

Free! Sarong's new booklet "Facts About Figures".
Write Sarong, Inc., Department MC-1, 200 Madison Avenue, New York 16, N. Y.

SARONG is the registered trademark
of Sarong, Inc. for its girdles."

sarong
the patented girdle

with the criss-cross front

Sarong, 1956

Sweethearts in Swimsuits

For you...
and the one who
makes your
temperature rise...
Catalina look-alike
swimsuits!

Shown here—
a fabulous
Signature Fabric
from the land of
the Pharaohs.
See Catalina
Sweetheart Sets
also in Clansman's Plaid,
Dalmatian and
other fascinating
patterns.

Ladies' swimsuit:
Pharaoh's Darling—$10.95.

Men's sport set:
Sudan shirt—$6.95;
Sudan 3-row boxer—$4.95.

For name of nearest
store, write: Sweethearts,
Catalina, Inc., 443 So. San Pedro
Los Angeles 13
© Catalina, Inc., a division of
Julius **KAYSER** & Company
hosiery · lingerie · gloves

Catalina

Tan with Tartan

Put some romance
in your "loaf life"!

ARROW
➤➤➤➤

Bali Cay

Whether you're taking a cruise to the Caribbean or just a week-end jaunt to the beach, do it with a splash! Add some *color* to the landscape; pick up an armful of Arrow *Bali Cays!*

These beauties are as colorful as a coral reef... and just as washable! They come in big, splashy patterns and small, neat designs in both cotton and rayon fabrics. In short or long sleeves. And all have the amazing Arafold Collar. Prices about $4.50 and up. (Subject to government regulation.) See *Bali Cay* at your Arrow dealer's now!

Cluett, Peabody & Co., Inc., Arrow Shirts · Sports Shirts · Ties · Handkerchiefs · Underwear.

Arrow Shirts, 1952

Catalina Sport Sets

NORM VAN BROCKLIN AND
ELROY "CRAZYLEGS" HIRSCH

Norm Van Brocklin and Crazylegs Hirsch form one of football's greatest passing teams.

Recently, they teamed up in another way—to select for you a special collection of Catalina beachwear. The garments they chose represent the finest in fabric, workmanship and value—and both athletes agreed that the styles are bold and masculine!

"Dig That Crazy Shirt," printed cotton sport set, with trunks that cuff in matching print, $13.95.

String-knit cotton T-shirt, in beige & white, grey & white, navy & white, $3.95. Walking shorts, linen weave, in natural, navy, brown or grey, $8.95.

Signature Print sport shirts: "Fireman Save My Child" (top), red or blue combinations, $6.95. "Good Morning" (left), white or navy background, $6.95; "On the Go" (right), black or navy, $6.95.

Lastex trunks (top), "Tropicana" California Hand Print, brown or blue, $4.95. Standard boxer trunks (left), tailored to trim your figure, five colors, $4.95. Novelty print trunks (right), in combinations of blue, brown or charcoal, $3.95.

Van Brocklin, right, is wearing "Jungle Rhythm" (in combinations of brown or blue, $12.95). Hirsch is wearing "Check 'N Double Check" (in navy and white or brown and white, also $12.95).

For name of nearest store, write: Catalina, Inc., Dept. R, 443 So. San Pedro St., Los Angeles 13.

Catalina, 1954

Catalina, 1952

Flip yourself into a Jantzen Reversible!

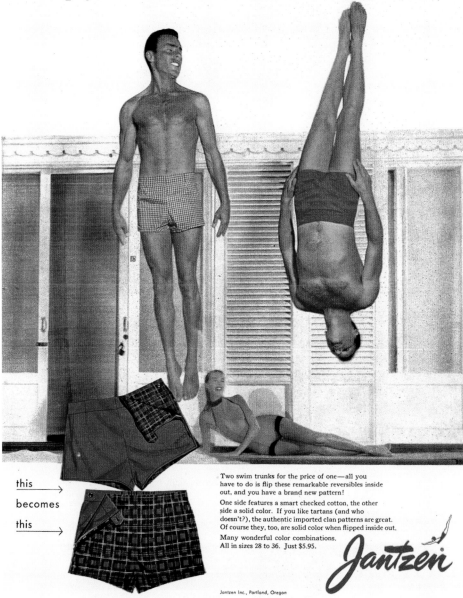

this →

becomes

this →

Two swim trunks for the price of one—all you have to do is flip these remarkable reversibles inside out, and you have a brand new pattern!

One side features a smart checked cotton, the other side a solid color. If you like tartans (and who doesn't?), the authentic imported clan patterns are great. Of course they, too, are solid color when flipped inside out.

Many wonderful color combinations. All in sizes 28 to 36. Just $5.95.

Jantzen

Jantzen Inc., Portland, Oregon

Jantzen, 1956

FABRIC BY RAYFLE

swimsuit by Cole of California Beautiful, isn't it? A rainbow of Coloray pastels that live forever! No fading ever in sunlight or under water, including soap and water! Because all the color comes from Courtaulds Coloray, the fiber that's most colorfast to all color dangers. Swimsuit of elasticized Coloray-acetate-cotton in sizes 32 to 38. About $22.95. At B. Altman & Co., New York; Marshall Field, Chicago; Neiman-Marcus, Dallas and Houston; Woolf Bros., Kansas City; Frederick & Nelson, Seattle; Henry's, Wichita, or write Courtaulds (Alabama) Inc., 600 Fifth Ave., N. Y. 20.

Coloray, 1958

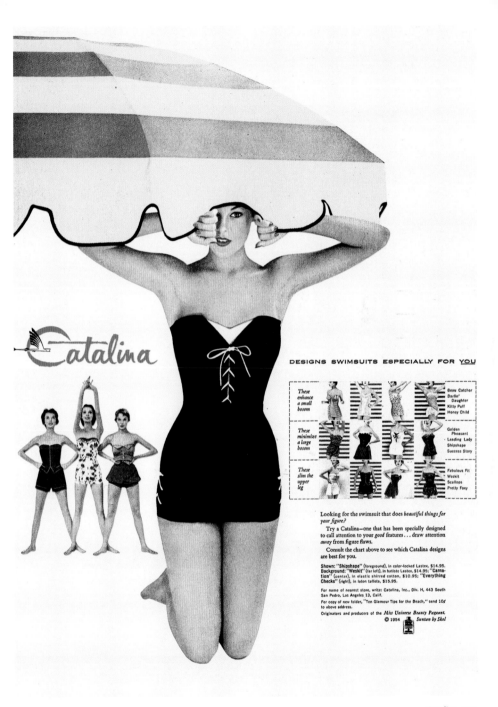

Catalina

DESIGNS SWIMSUITS ESPECIALLY FOR YOU

These enhance a small bosom					Beau Catcher Darlin' Daughter Kitty Puff Honey Child
These minimize a large bosom					Golden Pheasant Leading Lady Shipshape Success Story
These slim the upper leg					Fabulous Fit Weskit Scallops Pretty Foxy

Looking for the swimsuit that does *beautiful things for your figure?*

Try a Catalina—one that has been specially designed to call attention to your *good* features . . . draw attention *away* from figure flaws.

Consult the chart above to see which Catalina designs are best for you.

Shown: "Shipshape" (foreground), in color-locked Lastex, $14.95. Background: "Weskit" (far left), in batiste Lastex, $14.95; "Carnation" (center), in elastic shirred cotton, $10.95; "Everything Checks" (right), in faton taffeta, $15.95.

For name of nearest store, write: Catalina, Inc., Div. H, 443 South San Pedro, Los Angeles 13, Calif.

For copy of new folder, "Ten Glamour Tips for the Beach," send 10¢ to above address.

Originators and producers of the *Miss Universe Beauty Pageant.*

© 1954   *Suntan by Skol*

Catalina, 1954

Avondale, 1957

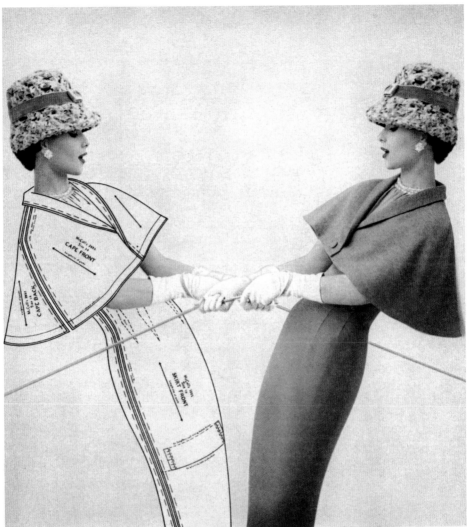

make the clothes that make the woman

Meet the leading look for spring: the dashing cape over the Empire sheath. Meet *our* version: wool and chiffon under gray-flecked tweed . . . the total in tones of violet. *You* might turn to apricot. Or why not blue for evening . . . the dress in shantung and voile, the cape in rich silk crepe? Do it our way . . . do it your way. But do it the easiest way: McCall's Easy Rule® feature lets you fit without fussing! Before you buy so much as a box of pins . . . check McCall's. Our March Pattern Catalog is at fine stores now . . . with patterns designed just for McCall's by Givenchy, Trigère, Galanos, Emilio of Capri!

remember: better fabrics make better fashions

McCall's
PRINTED PATTERNS
A DIVISION OF McCALL CORPORATION

McCall's, 1957

SUNLIGHT GIVES ZEST TO EVERYTHING...from cook-outs to cottons!
And Dan River Sunshades seem to have sunlight woven right in!
Colors and patterns radiate a special glow you've never
seen in cottons. Plaids, checks, stripes and embroideries
have fresh new fashion appeal. And these rare cottons
are Wrinkl-Shed! Wrinkles hang out overnight;
colors stay in for life. Designs are woven in! Ask
for Dan River Sunshade cottons in fashions for the
whole family, and by the yard. At all fine stores.

DAN **R**IVER
cottons in radiant ne
SUNSHADES

they're **Wrinkl·SHED***

Dan River, 1957

Tred-Lite
for men
$3.98

Tred-Lite
for women
$3.49

Tred-Lite
for boys
$3.49

Tred-Lite
for
children
$3.29

SEE HOW LITTLE TRED-LITES COST FOR THE ENTIRE FAMILY

Surprisingly less than you'd expect! The whole family
can step out together and stay within the budget
. . . in these carefree casuals that put a soft,
deep-yielding cushion between your foot and the
ground. In many styles and many colors . . . for work
and play . . . shoes that wear a long,
long time and cost so very little.

Prices slightly higher Denver West

Tred-Lite®

by **Cambridge**

CAMBRIDGE RUBBER COMPANY, CAMBRIDGE, MASS.

Fashion...a man's world, too

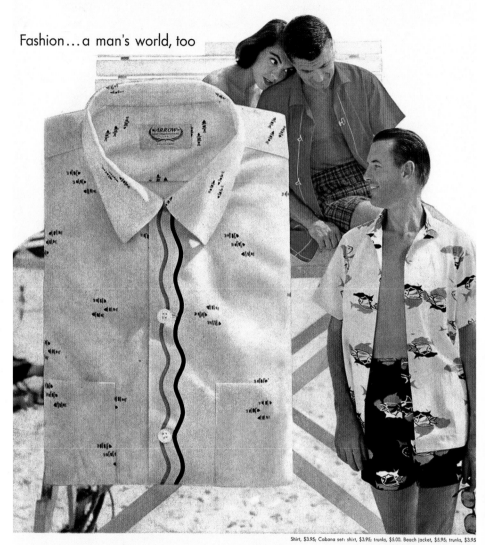

Shirt, $3.95; Cabana set: shirt, $3.95; trunks, $5.00. Beach jacket, $5.95; trunks, $3.95

We owe a thank-you note to Nassau. Our stylist stopped off there and was inspired to design these handsome prints for surf and sand. Patterns like these, on completely washable, "Sanforized" cotton, show the bold look men favor in their beach wear. It's no wonder you'll find Arrow Casual Wear worn at resorts wherever men prize distinctive styling.

ARROW — first in fashion

CASUAL WEAR

Cluett, Peabody & Co., Inc.

Give your beau an Arrow

Now you can be cooler than she is!

This is the age of

Wings

LIGHTWEIGHT SPORT SHIRTS FOR MEN AND BOYS

Galey & Lord combed yarn gingham
plaid, unconditionally washable $3.95.
Boys' Jr. sizes $2.95. Prep sizes $3.50.

Flightweight, combed cotton leno,
exclusive Wing-free pockets $2.95.
Boys' sizes $1.95.

Cool no-iron cotton crinkle, pin-
picked trim $2.95. Boys' Jr. sizes
$2.50. Prep sizes $2.95.

Sheer 100% Dupont nylon open weave $3.95.
Boys' Jr. sizes $2.95. Prep sizes $3.50.

Tri-Tone rayon linen shirt $2.95.
Denim Player shorts $2.50.

Seercheck, breezy acetate-Bemberg,
famous Wings no-iron crinkle $2.95.
Boys' sizes $2.50.

Washable linen-like rayon exclusive
anchor motif $3.95. Boys' sizes $2.95.

At value minded stores everywhere or write: WINGS • 4 W. 33rd St., New York 1

For the Motorist of Every Age...

the

MOTORIST COAT

by

BUCK SKEIN BRAND®

This is the age of the motorist...but whether you're driving, riding or walking, you'll want to be wearing the most comfortable coat ever designed.

To mention a few highlights...the sleeves are set in for power steering ease—never bind or restrict your movements. The quilted Estron lining covered in colorful stripes keeps you warm and comfortable in even the coldest weather. And, when you slip behind the wheel, you'll discover that the coat is motor-length ...never impedes or hampers you.

Leave it to Buck Skein Brand designers to fashion it handsomely of 100% pure wool—for nothing has ever equalled wool for warmth.

$27.95

PRICES SLIGHTLY HIGHER FAR WE

Buck Skein Brand, 1956

RONALD REAGAN
starring in
"BEDTIME FOR BONZO"
a Universal-International
Picture

BILLY ECKSTIN
Famous singin
Star of
"THE BIRD CAGE
and featured c
many MGM
record hits.

"JERIS rates cheers for **greaseless good grooming** and **healthier, handsomer hair**"

says *Ronald Reagan*

ONLY DANDRUFF-DESTROYING* JERIS HAS THIS FRESH, CLEAN-SCENTED MASCULINE FRAGRANCE

Of all the hair tonics on the market, JERIS and only JERIS brings you all these hair benefits:

1. *Greaseless good grooming.*

2. *Healthier, handsomer hair.*

3. *Scalp-stimulation:* Daily JERIS massage helps promote healthy hair growth, relieves dry scalp, excessive falling hair.

4. *Destroys dandruff germs* on contact:* antiseptic action *instantly* removes ugly dandruff flakes.

5. *Exclusive masculine fragrance:* daily use of JERIS leaves hair clean-scented. Economical, too! Get JERIS today at drug counters—professional applications at barber shops—everywhere.

JERIS is not greasy to the touch, won't discolor coat collars, can't soil shirts, stain hats or upholstery. For greaseless good grooming insist on JERIS Hair Tonic.

When George's dome was greasy
The dames shooed him away.
He switched to greaseless JERIS
He's a glamour
boy, today!

JERIS KILLS DANDRUFF GERMS* ON CONTACT. *Pityrosporum ovale, which many authorities recognize as the cause of infectious dandruff is destroyed by Jeris Antiseptic Hair Tonic.

JERIS
ANTISEPTIC HAIR TONIC

JERIS gets my applause for **GLOSSY GOOD GROOMING,** and **HEALTHIER, HANDSOMER HAIR,**

says Billy Eckstine

ONLY DANDRUFF-DESTROYING* JERIS HAS THIS FRESH, CLEAN-SCENTED MASCULINE FRAGRANCE

Of all the hair tonics on the market, JERIS and only JERIS brings you all these hair benefits: 1. *Glossy good grooming.* 2. *Healthier, handsomer hair.* 3. *Scalp-stimulation:* Daily JERIS massage helps promote healthy hair growth, relieves

dry scalp, excessive falling hair. 4. *Destroys dandruff germs* on contact*, antiseptic action *instan* removes ugly dandruff flakes. 5. *Exc sive masculine fragrance:* daily use Jeris leaves hair clean-scented. Get Je today at drug counters—professio applications at barber shops everywhe Jeris is not greasy to the touch, wo discolor coat collars, can't soil shir stain hats or upholstery. For greasel good grooming insist on Jeris Hair Tor

JERIS KILLS DANDRUFF GERMS* ON CONTACT.
*Pityrosporum ovale, which many authorities recognize as the cause of infectious dandruff is destroyed by Jeris Anti-septic Hair Tonic.

JERIS
ANTISEPTIC HAIR TONIC

23

Jeris, 1951

Jeris, 1950

Here's the
LONG
and the
SHORT
of it...

LB MAKES EVERY
HAIR STYLE
Look Better

Campus favorite
for guys...*and gals!*

L.B. BUTCH WAX
Hair control for
teen-age cuts and
all stubborn hair;
helps while
it trains.

Hair Cream
New and wonderful!
Lanolin-rich, non-
greasy dressing
in plastic
squeeze bottle.

L.B. POMADE
(with Lanolin)
Tops for weekly
massage, daily
grooming! Adds
life and lustre
to the hair.

L.B. OIL for the Hair
Lanolin-rich, all-
purpose conditioner;
basic hair-care for
men, women,
children.

L. B. MEANS LOOK BETTER
BETTER LOOK FOR L. B. }
WHEREVER TOILETRIES ARE SOLD!
L. B. LABORATORIES, GLENDALE, CALIFORNIA

L.B. Laboratories, 1959

The Pin-Curl Spray

'SATIN-SET'

WITH

Humidex

Revlon

POSITIVELY CONTAINS NO LACQUER

everybody loves a gift by

SHULTON

for him   for her

OLD SPICE GIFT SET
After Shave Lotion, After Shave
Talcum and Men's Cologne 3.00

OLD SPICE
Pre-Electric Shave
Lotion 1.00

ESCAPADE "FRAGRANCE KEYS"
Toilet Water and Dusting Powder 3.50

ESCAPADE
Spray Cologne 2.50

FRIENDSHIP GARDEN
Spray Cologne 2.50

FRIENDSHIP GARDEN "CHARMER"
Guest sizes of Toilet Water, Bubbling Bath
Crystals, Talcum, Body Sachet 1.25

OLD SPICE
After Shave Lotion
1.00 and 1.75

NEW! "THE CAPTAIN'S BOX"
Old Spice After Shave Lotion, After Shave
Talcum, Men's Cologne, Hair Groom Tonic
and Spray Deodorant 5.00

**Early American
OLD SPICE**
Dusting Powder 1.40

Early American OLD SPICE GIFT SET
Bubbling Bath Crystals and Toilet Water 2.50

OLD SPICE "TREASURE CHEST"
Pressurized Smooth Shave, After Shave Lotion,
Men's Cologne, After Shave Talcum, Men's
Shower Soap, Stick Deodorant, Body Talcum 7.00

DESERT FLOWER
Spray Perfume 3.50

DESERT FLOWER GIFT SET
Hand and Body Lotion, and Toilet Water 2.75

Prices plus tax, except on Pre-Electric Shave Lotion, soap, and shaving creams.

Watch "THE EVE ARDEN SHOW" every week on CBS-TV

PRODUCTS ALSO AVAILABLE IN CANADA

Revlon, 1957 ◄   *Shulton, 1957*   ►► *American Optical Company, 1959*

Through 125 years…

Grandma's "Specs" Have Become

When American Optical first started making silver-framed glasses in 1833, folks didn't think about how the *frames* looked. They were just downright glad to see better.

But how things have changed. Today,

glasses not only help you see better, bu American Optical frames are smart fashion acces sories … designed by stylists as carefully as Paris original. Frames are scientifically soun and glow with fashion's warmest colors . .

BETTER VISION FOR BETTER LIVIN

FRAME SHOWN ON MODEL — PRELUDE   LEFT ROW — TOP TO BOTTOM — ILLUSION, ROYAL GAYMONT, PERT   RIGHT ROW — TOP TO BOTTOM — GAYMONT, ROYAL CLIC, CUE,

Today's Fashion Showpieces

gleam with sparkling trim. Best of all, American Optical frames flatter your eyes . . . compliment your coloring . . . really *do* something for you.

You can obtain these new American Optical Showpieces anywhere in America through the Eye Care Professions.

RED DOT An AO exclusive.

Do your glasses loosen and slide around after a month's wear? Well, *not* if they are the new American Optical frames. These Red Dot frames have a unique "never loosen" construction which keeps them always in place, in comfort.

American ⬥ Optical
COMPANY
SOUTHBRIDGE, MASSACHUSETTS

SLIM SLACKS SHOWN WITH ESQUIRE'S "BRIGHT LIGHT" COLORS FEATURED FOR '55

The slim line in slacks takes over

Biggest single trend of '55 in men's clothing is the natural slim line from head to heel. This clean, straight cut completely replaces the rippling roominess of yesteryear's sportswear—puts your full-cut slacks among the family antiques. The time is ripe. Put on this lean, attractive look in dress slacks and inexpensive washable pants. You'll find that the good buy in *any* price bracket is equipped with the equally streamlined Talon trouser zipper.

Talon
REG U S PAT OFF
THE QUALITY ZIPPER

TALON, INC., MEADVILLE, PA. • IN MEXICO, CIERRE RELAMPAGO S. A DE C V. • IN CANADA, LIGHTNING FASTENER COMPANY, LIMITED

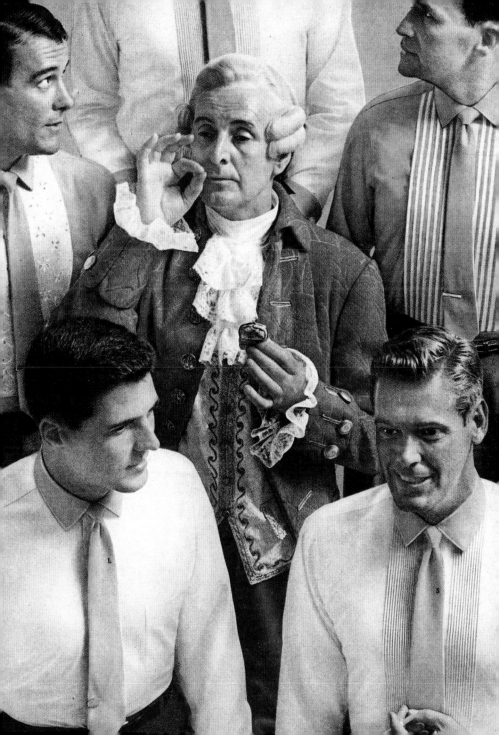

NO HELP NEEDED

Your New PERMA·LIFT BARE-BACK Bra
hooks in front—so quick—so easy

Lucky girl—you can forget all about those exasperating struggles with elusive back fastenings, for darling, those days of twisting, turning, reaching are all behind you. This chic new "Perma·lift"* Bare-Back Bra hooks in front—quickly, easily—without fuss or nonsense. And the clever, little hooks will never show—even through your clingiest, slinkiest dress. Be comfortably fitted today.

Style No. 88—Exclusive Criss-Cross** design keeps your Bare-Back Bra comfortably in place always. And Magic Insets in the cups support you from below In Dacron, only $8.95. In "D" cup—$10.00.

*Reg. U. S. Pat. Off. · **Pat. Applied For · A product of A. Stein & Company · Chicago—New York—Los Angeles*   *Prices may be slightly higher west of the Rockies*

Perma-lift, 1957

I dreamed I was a Work of Art in my *maidenform bra*

Maidenform, 1956

Obviously, the lady doesn't know

Perma·lift's Magic Oval Pantie

CAN'T RIDE UP—EVER!

Obviously the uncomfortable young shopper on your right doesn't know that "Perma·lift's"* Magic Oval Pantie** Can't Ride Up—Ever! Tugging at a girdle is so awfully necessary with ordinary garments. But this can't happen to you when you wear a "Perma·lift" Magic Oval Pantie, for it's actually guaranteed to remain in place always. Be fitted today.

Pantie 3844—Power Net with front and back control. Only $5.95.
Bra 132—Fine cotton with Magic Insets. $2.50.

TYLE No. 143:
, B and C CUPS

beautiful fit
is priceless

...yet the millions who wear Biflex
buy it for only $100

Biflex

BRAS AND GIRDLES

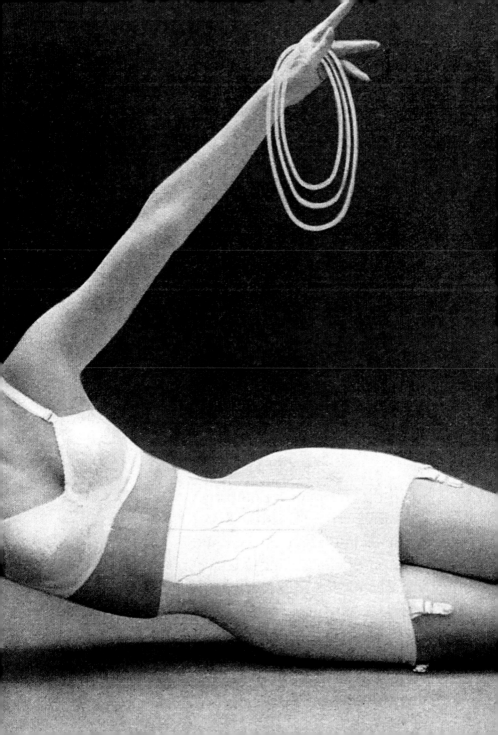

GUARANTEED

FRUIT OF THE LOOM
UNDERWEAR ®

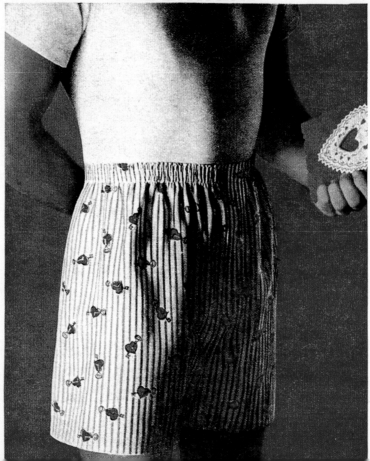

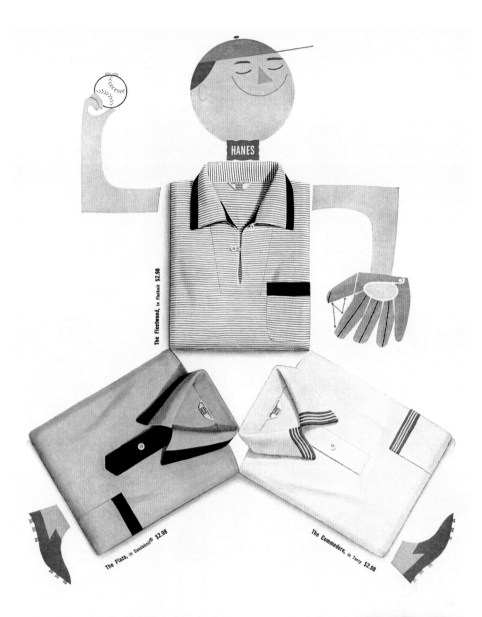

The Fleetwood, in Flatknit $2.98

The Plaza, in Suedeknit® $2.98

The Commodore, in Terry $2.98

Outdoor comfort comes in many colors. Stretching, jumping, bending, running, crawling, kneeling, bouncing, leaping, springing, vaulting or catapulting—you want a shirt that moves when you do. This is it. Hanes sport shirts, knit from colorful, colorfast cotton, are cashmere-soft and a breeze to wear. Crew-neck shirts need no ironing. Reinforced collars stay neat as new. Short sleeves. Cigarette pocket. Size-fast. At all good stores. Remember . . . to get more than you bargained for, be sure the name's . . .

P. H. Hanes Knitting Co., Winston-Salem 1, N.C.

HANES

ESQUIRE : June

Call Western Union by number in the cities listed on page 149 and ask for Operator 25 to learn where to buy this merchandise

143

SPORTSWEAR FOR EVERYWHERE • INSPIRED IN OREGON

It's only fair to tell you . . . you'll want a dozen different Pendleton skirts and sweaters this year. Such exciting variety!
All virgin wool . all with the fashion, fit and finish Pendleton's famous for! Figure-trimming or flared-for-freedom; panels
or pleats, sheaths or wraparounds, and the original Turnabout®* reversible . . . 12 marvelous skirt styles, $12.95-$29.95.
And to top it all, choose from a wealth of 17 dressmaker or casual sweaters, $7.95-$17.95, color-right for every skirt.

*Pat. No. 2530678

there is only one

Pendleton® Sportswear

always virgin wool

favorite pajamas that bring the family together

Individually Gift Packaged

FIRST NIGHTER

Whether your evening plans include a "do-it-yourself" project...TV, or good sleeping, you'll feel comfortable in these soft cotton knit tops, broadcloth slack-tailored trousers. Pastels or deep ton Dad's sizes A B C D, about $5.00; sizes E & Mr. Long, about $5.50. Son's sizes 4 to 20, about $3.95.

Be well turned out when you turn in

WELDON
PAJAMAS

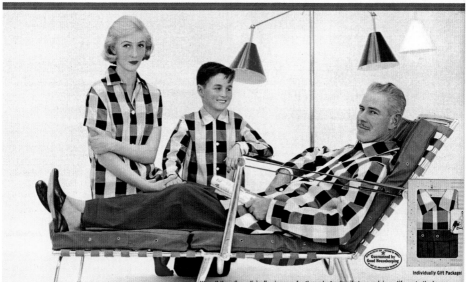

Individually Gift Packaged

CLUB LOUNGE

We call them "easy living" pajamas — for they adapt as easily to your leisure life as to the hours you spend sleeping. Smartly styled pajamas with leisure shirts, well-fitting, slack-tailored trousers. New color combinations. Mother's sizes with long or short sleeves, 32 to 40 (12 to 20), about $6.95. Dad's sizes with long sleeves, A B C D E & Mr. Long, about $7.50. Son's sizes Junior 4 to 12, about $3 Prep 13 to 20, about $5.00; little sister sizes 4 to 14, short sleeves, about $3.95.

WELDON PAJAMAS, EMPIRE STATE BUILDING, NEW YORK 1, N. Y.

Christmas just isn't Christmas without a family... of Dobbs hats.

Family man, sportsman, businessman. For all his interests there's the perfect Dobbs hat. Our many-sided man, below, is wearing a Dobbs velour Tyrolean. $20. (Ornaments extra.) There's the new Dobbs Two-Tone* Gamebird. Unique for town and country. $15. For evenings, the sophisticated Dobbs Black Homburg. $13.50 to $20. This year make his Christmas a Dobbs Christmas. Dobbs hats available at fine stores throughout the United States. Also Canada. $10.95 to $100. Dobbs, Park Ave. at 49th St., N.Y.
*U. S. Pat. #2,844,823 and other patents pending.

Dobbs is so easy to give when you give him a Dobbs gift certificate. Let him choose the style and color he wants. Dobbs gift certificates come packaged with unusual miniature Santa Claus cap.

DOBBS IS A DIVISION OF HAT CORPORATION OF AMERICA

Dobbs Hats, 1958

NEW SPRING RAYONS AND BLENDS STOP TRAFFIC, START SALES WITH <u>CO-ORDINATED</u> COLORS!

The proven success of color co-ordination has made it the big thing again this Spring! And Riegel puts it to work for you, in rayons and blends that will help make multiple sales of shirts, slacks, and shorts . . . on *sight*! See the wonderful range of colorful fabrics: rayons, Dacron*-and-cotton blends, "wash-and-wears" . . . linen weaves and prints. It's a complete new-for-Spring line that has everything you need for volume selling. Get going with Riegel rayons and blends!

IT'S A **Riegel** FABRIC

*Trademark

Riegel
COTTONS AND SYNTHETICS
SPINNING • WEAVING • FINISHING

RIEGEL TEXTILE CORP. • 260 Madison Avenue • New York 16, New York • ATLANTA • BOSTON
CHARLOTTE • CHICAGO • DALLAS • JACKSON (MISS.) • LOS ANGELES • ST. LOUIS

Riegel, 1955

Turning leaves splash the

Autumn scene with spectacular

hues...inspire new shirts with

subtle stripes, lavish plaids in the

COLORS OF INDIAN SUMMER

...for the look of the leader

McGregor captures the brilliant changing landscapes of Fall
—reaps a harvest of warm, glowing color—in a magnificent
new shirt collection of luxurious, washable cotton by Dan River.
(left) Kernel III—button-down, back-button, back-pleat Ivy
Leaguer. $6.95. (right) Kernel II—new soft roll collar. Fine plaid
on distinctive stripes. $6.95. (center) Kernel VI—
woven-cotton pullover with fashion-knit collar. $6.95.

Lamb Fleece Cru Sweaters in the
colors of Indian Summer.
75% luxurious lambswool for warmth
without weight—25% rugged Orlon
for washability, authentic crew-
neck...terrific colors!
Men's $7.95.
Wee $4.98.
Prep $5.98.

McGREGOR

SPORTSWEAR

Also boy-sized, boy-priced
McGregor-Doniger Inc., 303 5th Ave., New York 16, N. Y.   *T.M.

HOLIDAY/OCTOBER

McGregor, 1957

▶ *McGregor, 1951*

now! *Magnificent McGregor sweaters crafted for sweater collectors of every age... and every class— from '17 to '73!*

TRU-CRU SWEATERS... for the look of the leader

| s of '73—SEAFOAM | Class of '70—FIRE BELL | Class of '67—STORM CLOUD | Class of '62—GOLD NUGGET | Class of '56—VIN ROUGE | Class of '45—PACIFIC SKY | Class of '17—CORDOVAN |

*New intimate blend of imported lambswool (for silky softness) and Shetland (for durability)...
Result: warmth-without-weight elegance—in exclusive connoisseur colors!*

Inspired new colors! Authentic crew neck! Ruggedly warm! Light-weight! Designed for discriminating sweater collectors of all ages—from grad-Dad to pre-prep lad. Men's Tru-Cru $10.00. For men of the future $8.98.
NEW PENCIL-STRIPE SHIRTS—back-button, button-downs in pencil-thickness stripes... *fine-line, soft, medium, hard.* Men's $5.95. School-pencil shirts for the future man $3.98.

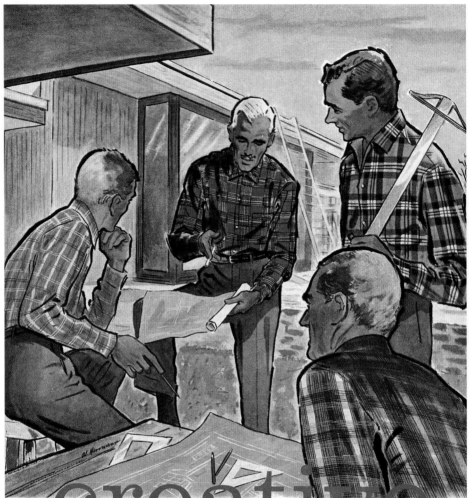

creative
...LIKE THE MEN WHO WEAR THEM

GALEY AND LORD EXCLUSIVES BY TRUVAL! Men of imagination...blue-printing a dream. And creative in their own right are these Galey and Lord plaids, designed especially for Truval and meticulously tailored. All are completely washable. Left: bold pattern, contrasting satin weave. Next: forceful plaid with woven ombre corners. Then: muted weave with satin stripe. Lower right: self-colored ombre, flowing from soft to deep. Choose your colors! Each 4.95. At fine stores or write: Truval Shirt Company, Empire State Bldg., New York, N.Y.

shirts · sportshirts · pajamas
Truval ®

CAMPUS

News from Scotland— International Tweed Coat... magnificent orlon fleece lining. New leather trim, "Weather-Leash" closure $59.95. New Norther lambswool and Shetland sweater $10.00. Silk 'n' cotton sportshirt $10.00. Forstmann Benara luxury-wool flannel slack $25.00.

From Sweden—Polar Seagull Coat; Princeton striped nylon fleece reverses to Travis-woven nylon taffeta. Jumbo-knit collar and cuffs, wash 'n' wear $25.00. Shirt—Match Top Tartan buttondown $5.95. Slack—Ivy Haven Flannel, no pleats $15.00.

WIDE, WIDE WORLD

McGregor searched every corner of the globe—no matter how remote—for new, interesting fabrics—handsome, dashing designs. The Continent, the Tyrol, the East, the Arctic, Scandinavia...all represented on these pages.

Yes, the accent is definitely international... and with McGregor as translator, a whole new world of global-inspired fashion awaits your inspection!

McGREGOR*

McGregor, 1959

Soft Illusions... fantastically soft pumps that weigh less than five ounces..... have super-cushioned soles ...and fit like Naturalizers always do.

COMPLETELY FLEXIBLE

LESS THAN 5 OUNCES LIGHT

GOODYEAR AIRFOOT CUSHIONING

Soft Illusions
by Naturalizer

High or mid heels in
a variety of colors . . . in
gossamer-light glacé calf.
Also in Deldi silk suede.

Shoes illustrated, 13.95. Other styles 9.95 to 13.95. Higher Denver West and Canada.

Naturalizer

THE SHOE WITH THE BEAUTIFUL FIT ®

37

Jacqueline

PRETTIEST

SHOES

ANYWHERE

Jacquelines keep smart pace with your gadabout Fall calendar — take you from shopping to luncheon to theatre in the height of fashion, and the fit of luxury. Stalk-slim, petal-smooth suedes and calf-skins with the exciting detail that make them the season's most sought-after shoes . . . at the most sought-after prices!

9⁹⁵ to 11⁹⁵

some styles slightly higher

COAT BY LUNAY

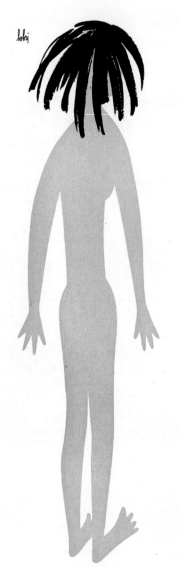

In 13000 BC
smart women
wore nothing.

In 1957 AD
smart women
wear nothing but
seamless
stockings
by
Hanes

no seams to worry about

TAKE TIME OUT FOR BEAUTY

avon cosmetics

Catalina's plot to get you
back to the sun! A daring
rounded U back in elasticised
lace sculptured into maillot lines.
Water Wisp — $25.00

Catalina®
LOVELIER BY DESIGN

Catalina, Inc., Los Angeles 13
Fine Swimwear and Sportswear
A division of Julius Kayser & Co.

THE HUE IS THE CRY!

sheer madness not to let
your legs share your colorful
costumes . . . sheer delight
when you choose Cameo's new
stocking tints. Left to right:
Sunburst, Flamingo, and Blue
Cloud, a sampling from
Cameo's collection of costume-
coordinated colors. $1.35 to
$1.65 a pair. Full-fashioned and
seamless—stretch, too.

bur-mil **cameo** stockings

Catalina, 1958 ◄

Cameo Stockings, 1958

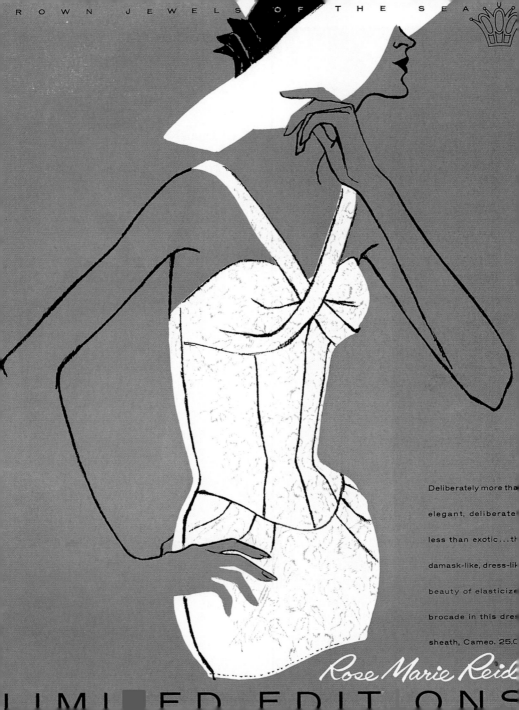

You, too, can make history. Wear stockings by **KAYSER**

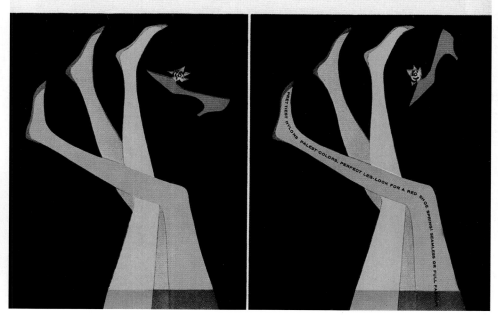

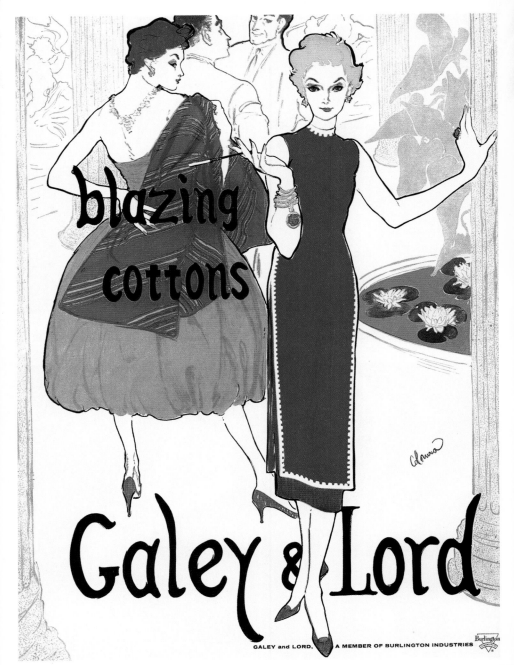

blazing cottons

Galey & Lord

GALEY and LORD, A MEMBER OF BURLINGTON INDUSTRIES

Galey & Lord, 1958

▶ *Cameo Stockings, 1958*

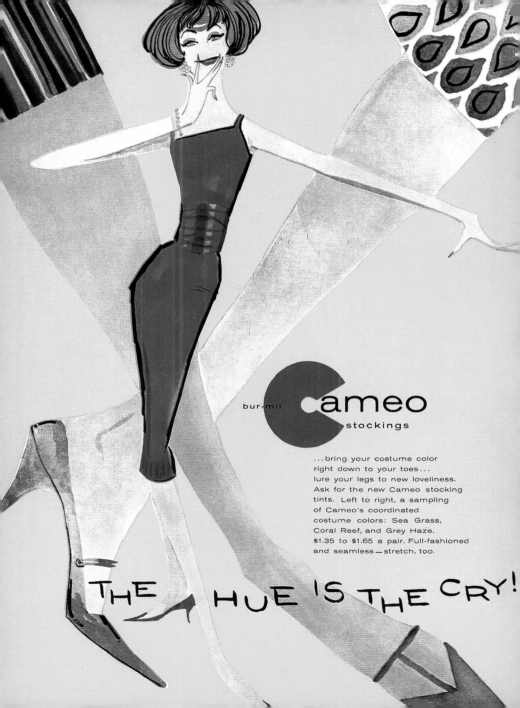

bur-mil **Cameo** stockings

...bring your costume color
right down to your toes...
lure your legs to new loveliness.
Ask for the new Cameo stocking
tints. Left to right, a sampling
of Cameo's coordinated
costume colors: Sea Grass,
Coral Reef, and Grey Haze.
$1.35 to $1.65 a pair. Full-fashioned
and seamless — stretch, too.

THE HUE IS THE CRY!

Coopers

A leading role every time in these "award-winning" Woven Shorts by Coopers. Comfortable, smooth fit with the Nobelt waistband that stays up firmly but gently. Washable cotton with famous U-Shape Construction that *never* binds! Choice of four colors. **Dollar-Fifty.** Other Boxer Shorts One Dollar Up.

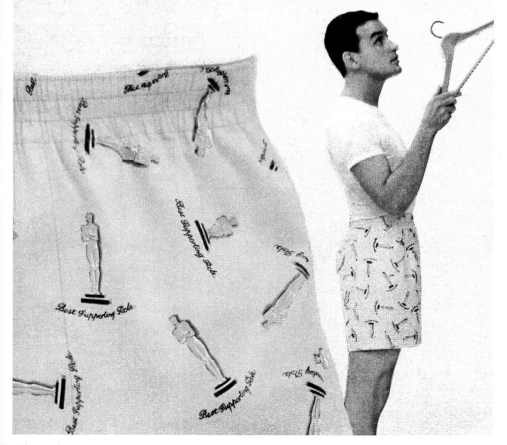